IN THE
FREUD ARCHIVES

PART I

PART I

I

In the mid-seventies, a young man named Jeffrey Moussaieff Masson began to appear at psychoanalytic congresses and to draw a certain perplexed attention to himself. He was an analyst-in-training at the Toronto Institute of Psychoanalysis, but he wasn't like the other analytical candidates one sees at congresses—quiet and serious and somewhat cowed-looking young psychiatrists who stand about together like shy, plain girls at dances, talking to one another with exaggerated animation. Masson (to continue the metaphor) not only assiduously steered clear of the wallflowers but was dancing with some of the most attractive and desirable partners at the ball: with well-known senior analysts, such as Samuel Lipton, of Chicago; Brian Bird, of Cleveland; Edward Weinshel and the late Victor Calef, of San Francisco; and—the greatest catch of all—K. R. Eissler, of New York.

Masson was lively, inquisitive, brash, very talkative, anything but cowed. He was not a psychiatrist but a Sanskritist. He had become a tenured associate professor of Sanskrit at the University of Toronto at the age of thirty (by thirty-five he was a full professor), and he gave off a sheen of the intellectual big time that even those who disliked him from the start were grudgingly impressed by. He was good-looking in a boyish, dark, mildly Near Eastern way. (The photographs of Masson that were presently to appear in the *Times, Newsweek*, and *Time* make him look more exotic than he does in life, and a bit plump and spoiled.) At the congresses, Masson would sometimes be accompanied by his wonderfully intelligent, thin, elegant, mockingly witty wife, Terri; she stood out from the wives of analysts as Masson stood out from his fellow-candidates. Victor Calef, in recalling his first meeting with the dazzling Massons, at a congress of the International Psycho-Analytical Association in Paris in 1973, spoke of them as if speaking of the young Scott and Zelda Fitzgerald. "They were so beautiful, so brilliant, so delicious," Calef recalled. (And felt compelled to add, "She was smart as a whip.") At the Paris congress, Masson read a paper criticizing Erik Erikson's book on Gandhi—a paper that was much admired and was subsequently published in the *International Journal of Psycho-Analysis*. (While other candidates were still copying out exercises with inky fingers, Masson, with irritating precocity, was already delivering and publishing papers.) The following year, at the spring meeting of the American Psychoanalytic Association, in Denver, he read a paper entitled "Schreber and Freud," which caused a New York analyst in the audience named Leonard Shengold to rise and say, "I've never heard of this man, but he's a find. Canada has sent us a national treasure."

It was at the Denver congress that Masson and Eissler had their first, fateful meeting. Eissler was then (and remains) one of the grand old men of contemporary psychoanalysis. He is tall, gaunt, and unmistakably European. He speaks with an accent whose dominant tone of Viennese asperity is incongruously coupled with and (one realizes on closer acquaintance) rendered all but pointless by an underlying, insistent, almost pathological kindheartedness. There is a class of people, however, to whom this kindheartedness does not extend. These are the enemies of Sigmund Freud (as Eissler sees them), for whom he has nothing but fierce enmity and a kind of bewildered derision. Eissler has thin gray hair, very thick glasses, and a full mouth, whose flat, downward-curving upper lip is startlingly familiar: one has seen this mouth in German Expressionist art—on the faces of the writers and intellectuals in the drawings of Pascin, the paintings of Kokoschka, the photographs of Sander. Recently, speaking of his first meeting with Masson (whose letters he no longer answers), Eissler said bitterly, "I realize now that there was something already wrong. He came up to me in the lobby of the hotel and said 'Dr. Eissler?' How did he know who I was?" But (as Masson points out) how could it have been anyone *but* Eissler? Who else would have looked like that? Eissler stands out from American analysts the way a lady's slipper leaps out at you in the woods. When I met him for the first time, in his apartment on Central Park West, I, too, felt a shock of recognition.

Eissler's eminence in psychoanalysis rests on a vast under-pinning. He is a training analyst at the New York Psychoanalytic Institute and the author of several dozen brilliantly intelligent and quirky papers on such subjects as deviations from classical analytical technique, the treatment of schizophrenics, the treatment of delinquents, and the debate on vaginal orgasm. He is a scholar of profound erudition and prodigious industry, who has written book-length psychoanalytic studies of Goethe, Leonardo da Vinci, and *Hamlet,* as well as essays on literary, historical, and biographical subjects. (The Goethe book is 1,538 pages long.) He is an extraordinary clinician. And, finally, he is the Secretary (euphemism for head, originator, and only active member) of the Sigmund Freud Archives, an organization that started quietly and inconspicuously in the early nineteen-fifties and has since become the subject of growing controversy and acrimony—and even, improbably, of a thirteen-million-dollar lawsuit filed against it in April 1982 by Masson. In a 1974 paper entitled "On Misstatements of Would-Be Freud Biographers, with Special Reference to the Tausk Controversy," Eissler gives a history of the Archives:

> After the Second World War, at a time when there was little interest in Sigmund Freud's life history, a small group of psychoanalysts—Hartmann, Kris, Lewin, Nunberg, and myself—became alarmed by the fact that a large number of letters by Freud had been lost as a result of the ravages brought about by the war. It was feared that if no measures were taken, the surviving documentation of Freud's life would be dispersed all over the world, and most of it would be lost to future research. The need for a Sigmund Freud Archives was thus recognized. Subsequently, the Library of Congress agreed to accept as a donation all documents collected by the Archives, and to make them accessible to scholars after prearranged dates, to be determined by the Archives.

The dates set ranged from a few years after the time of the donation to the year 2102. Along with collecting documents for deposit in the Archives, Eissler undertook to interview all the surviving friends, colleagues, relatives, and patients of Freud he could find, making tape recordings of the interviews. As the collection of letters, manuscripts, publications, photographs, and tape recordings grew, attempts were made to pry open the closed doors of the Archives. Freud scholars beseeched Eissler to lift the restrictions, but he refused, arguing that they were necessary to reassure prospective donors and interviewees, who might otherwise think twice before handing over delicate material or speaking about intimate matters. Moreover, as Eissler wrote in a memorandum to the New York Psychoanalytic Institute in 1969, "by having the promise of the Archives that no publication was being planned, the contributor was assured that the Archives was not motivated by any self-seeking aims but merely by the desire to have the source material collected and preserved for future biographers and scholars." When contemporary Freud scholars and biographers protested that they were being discriminated against, Eissler was unmoved by their plight. In a footnote of magnificent weirdness in his book *Talent and Genius,* he wrote, "Those who are truly interested in the general question of the creativity of scientific geniuses, or in the general psychology of creativity, will not be deprived by this policy [of restriction], because there is outside the Archives a mass of material concerning other geniuses that has as yet remained untapped by research." In other words, the sensible contemporary Freud scholar should cash in his chips and find himself another, less well-protected genius—Newton, Galileo, and Mozart were three whom Eissler seriously proposed in conversation.

Talent and Genius, published in 1971, is itself a work of extreme eccentricity. It was written in response to another book, published two years earlier, entitled *Brother Animal: The Story of Freud and Tausk,* by Paul Roazen, which implicated Freud in the suicide, at the age of forty, of one of his early disciples, Victor Tausk. Roazen's book is trivial and slight. Its scholarship, like that of many other works of pop history, does not hold up under any sort of close scrutiny.

But, unlike most pop historians, whose sins against the spirit of fact go undetected because nobody takes the trouble to check up on them, Roazen had the misfortune to attract the notice of someone who was willing to go to any lengths to catch him out. In *Talent and Genius,* Eissler administers one of the most severe trouncings of one scholar by another in the annals of scholarly quarrelling. Like Superman rushing to the aid of a victim of injustice, Eissler hastened to defend Freud against what he believed "may properly be called the most brutal attack ever directed at him"—Roazen's insinuation that Freud was to blame for Tausk's death because, motivated by sexual and professional jealousy, he turned away from him at a crucial moment. Eissler had little trouble in routing his enemy; no one who reads Eissler's book can remain unconvinced of the insubstantiality of Roazen's thesis or of the unsoundness of his scholarship. But—and here is the rub—almost no one has read (*can* read) Eissler's book. It is an impenetrable thicket, a work of total disorganization and shapelessness, a maze of wandering thoughts, associations, notions, and meditations. This book, perhaps more than any of Eissler's other works, reflects his character: its singular mixture of brilliance, profundity, originality, and moral beauty on the one hand, and willfulness, stubbornness, impetuosity, and maddening guilelessness on the other.

Eissler's devotion to Freud is known throughout the analytic world, and is considered a kind of lovable nuttiness. Today's analysts have an admiring but somewhat cool attitude toward Freud. The popular picture of psychoanalysis as a religion of fanatical followers of Freud is far from a true one. Most Freudian analysts can take or leave Freud himself. Their interest in his life, and in the early history of psychoanalysis, is minimal, and their sensitivity to slurs on Freud's character is quite dulled. What Eissler sees as a "denigration" of Freud and a "desecration" of his memory other analysts are apt to shrug off, or even possibly take a little malicious pleasure in. Eissler's position as Defender of the Faith has caused rumors to circulate about him that range from the not improbable notion that he was a member of Freud's circle in Vienna in the thirties to an incredible tale of his having been adopted by Freud as a boy after the death of his father. But in fact, as Eissler writes in *Talent and Genius,* "I never met Freud, and I know little more about his life than does any reader who has studied the pertinent literature."

As Freud's archivist, Eissler inevitably came to have close dealings with Freud's daughter Anna, who took up Freud's mantle after his death and wore it until her own death, in October 1982. Eissler's idolatry of the father did not extend to the daughter. "She was not my type," he confessed to me during a recent conversation, and went on, "She was very strict, very German—more like a person from Hamburg than a Viennese. In the early days of the Archives, my contact with Anna Freud was very flimsy, very superficial. Gradually, I got closer to her, but, frankly, it was against my will. When we met, after the war, she was very mistrustful of me. I had offered to raise funds for her—for a Sigmund Freud Foundation at Hampstead [where the Freud family lived in London after their escape from the Nazis]—and for a long time she said no, I should not collect any money. I had the feeling that she was afraid of the price she might have to pay if I did her a favor. It's always dangerous to accept favors. And only after she found out that I would not ask her favors did she consent. I asked her only once for a favor—twice, maybe. No, once—in the matter of Masson I asked her for no favor; I just told her that he was reliable. She was very mistrustful of him, too, at first, but as time went on he impressed her with his ebullience, his juvenile high spirits. He is a permanent adolescent, and that infects you. It's very appealing and attractive. Anna Freud and I grew personally closer over the years, but we never became really close. I could never entirely relax in her presence—she was so animated by a sense of duty. And she was not emotional. I don't think I could have been in analysis with her. I would have been ashamed to tell her my fantasies—simply impossible. I have heard of one patient of Anna Freud's who on her way to treatment took off her lipstick. I understand that."

"Does it strike you as curious that Freud should have had a daughter with such a forbidding character?" I asked.

"Freud himself had a very strong superego," Eissler replied. "Fulfillment of duty was more important in his life than pleasure. But he had the faculty of enjoyment—which Anna Freud also had. That always touched me about her: her capacity for finding something beautiful and enjoyable in small things, like being taken out to dinner, or looking at a building."

"People say she was sexless," I said.

"I had the feeling of a great personality, not of an old maid. I once accompanied her to the house of a man who had given money to the Foundation—a very wealthy man with some terrible disease that had paralyzed him—and she listened to his complaints, and it was quite an experience. I've never seen anyone listen with such intensity. One gets a similar feeling from a home movie of Freud that shows him reading a magazine. His eyes have a colossal intensity of taking in. In both cases, one felt in the presence of someone for whom listening and reading were not passive but real actions. Also, her lecturing was superb. No notes, very clear, and always proceeding from one problem to another in a very appealing way. In her seminar, her clinical acumen was outstanding. But Anna Freud's writing does not have the depth and passion of Freud's. When reading Freud, one always feels that there is more there than actually is there. Anna Freud's writing does not have this quality. This is because— I'm sorry to say it—she was a woman; she was not a genius. When a genius writes, there is always so much more, and it is open to the whole world."

In contrast to the gradually and cautiously developing, and never totally satisfying, friendship of Anna Freud and Eissler, the friendship of Jeffrey Masson and Eissler took off like a rocket. When they met in Denver in 1974, the sixty-six-year-old analyst and the thirty-three-year-old candidate immediately hit it off. There had been some correspondence between them: long, deferential letters from Masson, asking for advice and enlightenment, and polite and encouraging replies from Eissler. But, unlike many relationships that begin and flourish in the benign, self-inventing atmosphere of letters and then wither in the rugged terrain of actuality, the friendship of Masson and Eissler was grounded in personal magnetism, in the attraction between their two personalities. The quality of the friendship does not come across in their decade of correspondence; the letters of neither have the intimacy, affection, emotion, and plain fun that colored their relationship. Eissler's letters remain somewhat stiff and staccato, betraying personal feeling only when he was irritated with his protégé and felt constrained to reprove him. Masson's letters retain their air of boyish deference and the A student's eagerness to show off. When they met, however— at psychoanalytical congresses or in Eissler's apartment in New York—the two men had a wonderful time, often staying up to talk past two in the morning. For Eissler, Masson was almost too good to be true. He embodied all that Eissler most cherished in people: intellect, erudition, energy, zest, color, sparkle, even a certain wildness—qualities that the early analysts evidently had in abundance but that today's sober practitioners entirely lack. During their late-night discussions, Masson would regale Eissler with horrid examples of the dullness, venality, and poor writing of American analysts, and Eissler—who was one of the first people within the profession to publicly deplore its medicalization, in a book called *Medical Orthodoxy and the Future of Psychoanalysis* (1965)—would listen entranced. Although he himself was more charitable—or, at any rate, more taciturn—about the cultural insufficiencies of his colleagues, he was not above hearing them retailed by his irrepressibly disdainful young friend. "It was very refreshing," Eissler recalls. "He spoke without hesitation. He had this nice, appealing, juvenile quality that I liked. What I call his hypomanic character was very stimulating." Eissler adds, "He had a very positive attitude toward Freud. There never was any indication that he did not think Freud was a great man."

For Masson, Eissler seemed a similar unbelievable stroke of good fortune. Masson was a practiced hand at seeking and winning the favor of older men in positions of power. As an undergraduate at Harvard, he had pressed himself on, and ultimately prevailed over the patrician reserve of, Daniel Ingalls, chairman of the Department of Sanskrit and Indian Studies; as a graduate student abroad, he had charmed the eminent French Sanskritist Louis Renou and the Belgian Buddhologist Étienne Lamotte; and now in the world of analysis he was again putting himself out for his elders and betters, and reaping the rewards of his eagerness to please and his ability to amuse. But Eissler was different from all previous mentors. None of them had wholeheartedly given himself over to Masson; each had held back some part of himself, refused some favor, failed some test of love. Eissler, incredibly, held back no part of himself, refused Masson nothing, loved him quite beyond all expectation. He gave him the greatest gift that it was in his power to bestow: he arranged to make him his successor as Secretary of the Freud Archives. And Masson, in return, fitted himself to the image that Eissler had formed of him. That things should have ended so badly between them was probably inevitable.

2

AT 11 a.m. on November 1, 1982, I came down to the lobby of the Claremont Hotel, in Berkeley, where I had arrived the night before, to meet Jeffrey Masson for the first time. A young-looking, well-built man with a mass of curly graying hair, wearing jeans and a denim jacket and tinted aviator glasses and carrying a leather shoulder bag, greeted me cheerfully and immediately confessed to a problem. Another woman whom it was important that he see had, as it happened, also arrived at the Claremont. Would it be all right if we sat in the lobby for a few minutes and waited for her? She was Alice Miller, a Swiss psychoanalyst and the author of a book entitled *Prisoners of Childhood,* which was a best-seller in Germany and had recently come out in translation here. Alice Miller, Masson explained, was his only remaining supporter. "I am persona non grata in the analytic world, a pariah," he said, with the air of one stating a mildly irksome and yet somehow not unamusing fact. He continued, with a rush of words, "Analysts won't speak to me anymore. They avoid me on the street. They are afraid to be seen with me. A year ago, they were fawning on me—they were giving me huge grants, they were inviting me to speak at their institutes. But when Anna Freud and Eissler dropped me no analyst would touch me. They see me as a dangerous person. They are terrified of my ideas. They are afraid I will destroy psychoanalysis—and they are right to be afraid. I have discovered that Freud wasn't honest. I'm writing a book called *The Assault on Truth: Freud's Suppression of the Seduction Theory*. And when my book comes out there is not a patient in analysis who will not go to his analyst with the book in hand and say, 'Why didn't you tell me this? What the hell is going on? I want an explanation. This man is telling me that there is something profoundly wrong at the core of psychoanalysis. Jesus Christ! If this is really true, what am I doing here?' When I was fired from the Archives, Alice Miller, who shares my ideas and therefore can no longer call herself a Freudian analyst either, was the only person who had the guts to come out for me. She sent me a telegram of support and got me a contract for my book with her German publisher. Her own book isn't very profound—it's not scholarly—but it's on the right track, and I owe her a great deal."

Alice Miller presently appeared—a small, worried-looking woman in her early sixties. Masson embraced her warmly, introduced me, and asked her what he could do for her during her stay in Berkeley. Alice Miller said that she wanted to know more about psychotherapy in America. "No problem," Masson said. "I'll arrange an evening meeting with local psychotherapists. Would forty people be enough? I'll call Danny Goldstine. He has a big house here in Berkeley—a mansion—and he'll be able to get a group together in a few days." Masson then asked Alice Miller how she was enjoying the Claremont—an enormous Victorian pile that had recently been refurbished and surrounded by an incongruously charmless landscape of parking lots, tennis courts, and swimming pools. Alice Miller said in an aggrieved tone that she had gone swimming in one of the pools and was having trouble with the chlorine in her eyes; the goggles sold at the hotel hadn't worked properly. She used a different kind of goggles in Switzerland, and they worked better. "Yes, yes," Masson said sympathetically. "I know the kind you mean. That's the only kind that really keeps the water out of your eyes. You should have that kind. I'll get you a pair today."

Masson looked at his watch, and said that if he and I were to get a table at Chez Panisse, the fashionable restaurant where he had proposed we lunch, we had better go. He arranged with Alice Miller to take her to see the Muir redwood forest the next morning, and we parted from her. As he and I walked through the lobby, he sighed and said, "Goggles, yet. God, she's kvetchy! She's like my mother. Where am I going to find goggles? Where am I going to find the time to look for goggles?"

We arrived at Chez Panisse at ten minutes to twelve, but a line had already formed on the narrow staircase leading to the second-floor dining room. Masson, undaunted, made his way to the maître d'hôtel and explained to him—as if it were the most reasonable and self-evident proposition in the world

—that he was being interviewed by someone from a magazine and therefore had to have a table right away, so the interview could proceed. He put forward this absurdity so nicely, pleasantly, and almost plausibly that only a very churlish person —or an experienced maître d'hôtel—could have refused him. The Chez Panisse maître d' refused him, but relented to the extent of giving us permission to sit in the empty downstairs dining room—used in the evening only—while we waited our turn, so that the interview could go forward.

I sipped a glass of wine and Masson a glass of Perrier, and he continued the story he had begun to tell me on the telephone a week earlier, when I called him from New York. I had first heard of Masson in the summer of 1981—as had other readers of the *Times*—when two long articles by Ralph Blumenthal appeared in the Science section. The first article, on August 18, was headed "SCHOLARS SEEK THE HIDDEN FREUD IN NEWLY EMERGING LETTERS," and the second, on August 25, ran under the headline "DID FREUD'S ISOLATION, PEER REJECTION PROMPT KEY THEORY REVERSAL?" The "newly emerging letters" were the one hundred and sixteen letters of Freud to Wilhelm Fliess that had been omitted from the edition of the Freud-Fliess correspondence published in 1950; Masson had received permission from Anna Freud to publish these missing letters in a new, complete edition of the correspondence. The "key theory" was the seduction theory, which Freud held between 1895 and 1897 and then dropped. This theory proposed that sexual abuse in infancy or earliest childhood was the root cause of hysteria, and traditional accounts of the emergence of psychoanalysis all agree that Freud's realization that his theory was wrong was the fulcrum of his momentous discovery of the cornerstones of psychoanalytic theory: infantile sexuality and the Oedipus complex. This victory-snatched-from-the-jaws-of-defeat version of the story derives from Freud himself. In his *An Autobiographical Study,* of 1925, he writes:

> Before going further into the question of infantile sexuality I must mention an error into which I fell for a while and which might have had fatal consequences for the whole of my work. Under the influence of the technical procedure which I used at that time, the majority of my patients reproduced from their childhood scenes in which they were sexually seduced by some grownup person. With female patients the part of seducer was almost always assigned to their father. I believed these stories, and consequently supposed that I had discovered the roots of the subsequent neurosis in these experiences of sexual seduction in childhood. My confidence was strengthened by a few cases in which relations of this kind with a father, uncle, or elder brother had continued up to an age at which memory was to be trusted. If the reader feels inclined to shake his head at my credulity, I cannot altogether blame him; though I may plead that this was at a time when I was intentionally keeping my critical faculty in abeyance so as to preserve an unprejudiced and receptive attitude towards the many novelties which were coming to my notice every day. When, however, I was at last obliged to recognize that these scenes of seduction had never taken place, and that they were only fantasies which my patients had made up or which I myself had perhaps forced on them, I was for some time completely at a loss. My confidence alike in my technique and in its results suffered a severe blow; it could not be disputed that I had arrived at these scenes by a technical method which I considered correct, and their subject matter was unquestionably related to the symptoms from

which my investigation had started. When I had pulled myself together, I was able to draw the right conclusions from my discovery: namely, that the neurotic symptoms were not related directly to actual events but to wishful fantasies, and that as far as the neurosis was concerned psychical reality was of more importance than material reality. I do not believe even now that I forced the seduction fantasies on my patients, that I "suggested" them. I had in fact stumbled for the first time upon the Oedipus complex, which was later to assume such an overwhelming importance, but which I did not recognize as yet in its disguise of fantasy.

In the Blumenthal articles, Masson was identified as one of a new generation of "critics" who believed that "Freud had it right the first time"—that the seduction theory was essentially correct, and that Freud's abandonment of it, far from being a triumph, was something of a disaster for psychoanalysis. The other New Critics cited by Blumenthal were two nonmedical, revisionist New York analysts, Milton Klein and David Tribich; a German sociologist, Marianne Krüll; and a French academic, Marie Balmary. Blumenthal found it "surprising" that Masson—"a prominent Freud archivist" and the "psychoanalyst selected by Anna Freud as director of the project to publish her father's complete letters to his closest confidant"—would hold such unorthodox views, and would even go so far as to say (in a lecture he had delivered in New Haven two months earlier, before the Western New England Psychoanalytic Society) that "by shifting the emphasis from a real world of sadness, misery, and cruelty to an internal stage on which actors performed invented dramas for an invisible audience of their own creation, Freud began a trend away from the real world that, it seems to me, has come to a dead halt in the present-day sterility of psycho-analysis throughout the world."

The Freudian establishment found it surprising, too. Two and a half months later, another article by Blumenthal appeared in the *Times*, with the headline "FREUD ARCHIVES RESEARCH CHIEF REMOVED IN DISPUTE OVER YALE TALK." It began, "A Berkeley scholar entrusted with private papers of Sigmund Freud has been removed as research director of the Sigmund Freud Archives in New York City after indirectly blaming Freud for 'the present-day sterility of psychoanalysis throughout the world.'" It went on to say, "The reaction culminated Thursday night in a vote by the 13-member board of the Freud Archives—a non-profit foundation controlling the vast public and private papers of Freud—not to renew Dr. Masson's contract as projects director for a second year starting in January. The board voted to offer him a year's pay, $30,000, as severance and in recognition of his scholarship." Eissler was quoted as saying, "Would you make director of the Archives someone who writes plain nonsense? He must foresee that he cannot get an honorary place here." Anna Freud "declined comment . . . when reached by telephone in London, except to say 'I regret this publicity.'" Masson, identified as a "non-practicing psychoanalyst and Sanskrit scholar who taught at the University of California at Berkeley," got off a memorable line. Speculating about the effect of the "new view of the seduction theory" on psychotherapy, he said, with inspired impudence, "They would have to recall every patient since 1901. It would be like the Pinto."

Now, at Chez Panisse, Masson looked back with alternating wonder, glee, and indignation at the rise and fall of his fortunes in the Faubourg Saint-Honoré of psychoanalysis. "The way to get one-up among analysts is to use the word

'Anna,' " he said. "Nobody ever called Anna Freud 'Anna' to her face, but they all pretended they did. They'd say, 'When I was with Anna at Hampstead.' Or, 'I know Kurt Eissler. When Kurt and I were talking the other day, he told me . . .' That sort of thing. Analysts are the worst name-droppers in the world. So, you see, it was a traumatic experience for American analysts to see a young guy like me lounging around Anna Freud's house and running around with hundreds of Freud's letters sticking out of his pockets and being doted on by Kurt Eissler, who was so distant and formal with everyone else. They felt that I had been taken up by Eissler and Anna Freud and other powerful members of the international analytical community very unfairly—not because of any objective qualities I had but because of a certain psychopathic personality charm. It incensed them. They would say to me, 'I have spent my life trying to get one letter of Freud's, and you go there and Anna Freud opens up her father's bloody desk to you. Why? Why you, you little son of a bitch? What did *you* ever do?' When I spoke at the Chicago analytic institute last year, there was actually a question like that from the audience. One of the senior analysts got up and said, 'I just want to ask one question. Why you? Who's ever heard of you? We never heard of you. You're not famous. You haven't written much. You're a nobody. Why should you get all those privileges and we get nothing?' "

"How did you answer that?" I asked.

"I said, 'Because I'm smarter than you'—which is true. 'Because I know more than you, and I've got more guts, and I asked for the privileges, and I'm very good at what I do.' But I don't know. I suppose the real answer is 'Because Eissler adored me, and Eissler was all-powerful with Anna Freud.'

Anna Freud would never have looked at me if it hadn't been for Eissler."

I asked Masson just how he had contrived to get Anna Freud's permission to publish the complete Freud-Fliess correspondence—a feat reminiscent of the (failed) scheme of the narrator of Henry James's *The Aspern Papers* to wrest the letters of the poet Jeffrey Aspern from the grasp of the old woman and her niece. The story of how the Freud-Fliess correspondence came to light is itself novelistic. Ernest Jones tells it in the first volume of his biography of Freud:

> Freud destroyed the letters Fliess had written to him, but Fliess preserved Freud's. Some time after Fliess's death in 1928, his widow sold the packet of 284 extremely private letters, together with the accompanying scientific notes and manuscripts Freud had from time to time sent him, to a bookseller in Berlin, Reinhold Stahl by name. But she sold them under the strict condition that they were not to pass to Freud himself, knowing that he would immediately destroy them. . . .
>
> Stahl fled to France for a while in the Nazi regime and there offered the documents to Mme. Marie Bonaparte, who at once perceived their value and acquired them for £100. She took them with her to Vienna, where she was doing some postgraduate analysis with Freud, and spoke of them to him. He was indignant about the story of the sale and characteristically gave his advice in the form of a Jewish anecdote. It was the one about how to cook a peacock. "You first bury it in the earth for a week and then dig it up again." "And then?" "Then you throw it away!" He offered to recompense Mme. Bonaparte by paying half of her expenses, but fearing this would bestow some right on him in the matter she re-

fused. She read to him a few of the letters to demonstrate
their scientific value, but he insisted that they should be
destroyed. Fortunately she had the courage to defy her
analyst and teacher, and deposited them in the Rothschild
Bank in Vienna during the winter of 1937–38 with the
intention of studying them further on her return the next
summer.

When Hitler invaded Austria in March, there was
the danger of a Jewish bank being rifled, and Mme.
Bonaparte went at once to Vienna where, being a princess
of Greece and Denmark, she was permitted to withdraw
the contents of her safe-deposit box in the presence of
the Gestapo; they would assuredly have destroyed the
correspondence had they detected it on either that occasion or earlier in Berlin. When she had to leave Paris for
Greece, which was about to be invaded, in February,
1941, she deposited the precious documents with the
Danish Legation in Paris. It was not the safest place, but
thanks to General von Choltitz's defiance of Hitler's
orders at the war's end, Paris, together with the Danish
Legation, was spared. After surviving all those perils, the
letters braved the fifth and final one of the mines in the
English Channel and so reached London in safety; they
had been wrapped in waterproof and buoyant material
to give them a chance of survival in the event of disaster
to the ship.

These letters, written between 1887 and 1902, are col-
lectively regarded as the single most important document of
the early history of psychoanalysis. Fliess was a Berlin nose-
and-throat specialist, two years younger than Freud, toward
whom Freud formed what in psychoanalytic terms is called
an idealizing transference, and with whom he shared all his
thinking during the (for psychoanalysis) critical decade of

the eighteen-nineties. A selection of a hundred and sixty-eight letters (from the total of two hundred and eighty-four) was made in 1950 by Anna Freud, Ernst Kris, and Marie Bonaparte, and was published, first in German and four years later in English, under the title *The Origins of Psychoanalysis*. The title is a very good one. From this book one indeed receives an awesome sense of being privy to the earliest stirrings of psychoanalytic thought, of witnessing the emergence, in all its rawness, newness, strangeness, and precariousness, of what was to become psychoanalysis. Reading the Freud-Fliess correspondence is like coming upon the earliest and roughest drafts of a great poem. From such records of the workings of the poetic imagination as we possess we have learned that poems do not, as a rule, arrive in a flash of inspiration but derive from much hard, stubborn, even somewhat prosaic work; drafts of poems are full of false starts, wrong turns, and dead ends as well as of cautious gropings, humble glimmerings, and dawning realizations. Freud's letters to Fliess similarly reveal that psychoanalysis did not spring from the head of Freud like Athena from the head of Zeus but was the product of years of characteristically perilous, error-fraught, uncomfortable, unpleasant creative struggle. The "error . . . which might well have had fatal consequences for the whole of my work," as Freud calls it in the *Autobiographical Study* (in *On the History of the Psycho-Analytic Movement* he calls it "a mistaken idea . . . which might have been almost fatal to the young science"), was part of a larger tendency in Freud's thought which was leading him astray in the eighteen-nineties—astray in the sense that it was not leading him toward psychoanalysis. This was the tendency to trace neurosis to disturbances of sexual life brought on by social and environmental evils. People, he

then believed, became hysterics, obsessional and anxiety neu-
rotics, melancholics, or neurasthenics (as the sufferers from
neuroses were then classified) either because of what had
been done to them in childhood by incestuous adults (the
seduction theory) or because of what they had to endure in
a society that was riddled with syphilis and gonorrhea, that
lacked any acceptable and reliable contraceptives, and that
was consequently pervaded by an atmosphere of sexual fear,
guilt, aversion, and disgust. In a draft of a paper that Freud
sent to Fliess in 1893, entitled "The Aetiology of the Neuroses," he cited *coitus interruptus, onanismus conjugalis,* and
masturbation as the unhappy but only alternatives to un-
wanted pregnancy and to venereal disease contracted from
prostitutes, all of which almost invariably led to neurosis. "It
follows from what I have said that the neuroses can be completely prevented but are completely incurable," Freud
wrote, and went on to gloomily conclude that "in the absence
of such a solution [he meant prophylaxis against venereal disease and "an innocuous method of preventing conception . . .
for the condom provides neither a safe solution nor one that
is tolerable to anyone who is already neurasthenic"], society
seems doomed to fall a victim to incurable neuroses which
reduce the enjoyment of life to a minimum, destroying the
marriage relation and bringing hereditary ruin on the whole
coming generation." He added lamely, "Thus the physician
is faced by a problem whose solution deserves all his efforts."
If Freud had continued his own efforts in this direction, he
would have become the inventor of a better condom, not the
founder of psychoanalysis. His gradual and reluctant shift of
focus from the miseries of the outer world to the woes, of a
different order, of the inner world is what is meant by the
"discovery of the unconscious."

The Freud-Fliess letters reveal the immense difficulty with which Freud negotiated his revolution from without to within; they document the resistance that accompanied each of his steps away from the familiar terrain of so-called objective reality to the uncharted wilderness of psychic reality. This resistance was never completely overcome by Freud—as it is never overcome by anyone. The most dedicated of Freudians do daily battle with the disinclination of the mind to accept the chastening evidence of the fossils of the unconscious (dreams, slips of the tongue, forgettings, accidents) in favor of the more acceptable testimony of the ordinary senses. The unexamined life may not be worth living, but the examined life is impossible to live for more than a few moments at a time. To fully accept the idea of unconscious motivation is to cease to be human. The greatest analyst in the world can live his own life only like an ordinary blind and driven human being. Like his patients, he receives occasional glimpses of the peculiar activities going on behind the curtain of consciousness; and, like his patients, he is always running a little behind. The crowning paradox of psychoanalysis is the near-uselessness of its insights. To "make the unconscious conscious"—the program of psychoanalytic therapy—is to pour water into a sieve. The moisture that remains on the surface of the mesh is the benefit of analysis.

From the resistance that even card-carrying Freudians put up against the Freudian unconscious, the resistance of the non- or anti-Freudians may be deduced. Writing of this resistance—as he frequently did—Freud said, in the *New Introductory Lectures,* of 1933, "You can believe me when I tell you that we do not enjoy giving an impression of being members of a secret society and of practicing a mystical science. Yet we have been obliged to recognize and express as our conviction that no one has a right to join in a discussion of psychoanalysis who has not had particular experiences which can only be obtained by being analyzed oneself." This reluctant conviction of Freud's has become a tradition within psychoanalysis. Outsiders wishing to join in the discussion of psychoanalysis—which they feel entitled to do as members of the therapeutic community to which we all belong because Freud lived and wrote—are, in effect, told to go away and maybe come back after they've been analyzed. Writers on psychoanalytic theory or history who come from other fields are regarded with suspicion and skepticism by those within the field. The worst is expected from them—and the worst very often comes. Writings about psychoanalysis from outside the field (with a few notable exceptions, such as Philip Rieff's *Freud: The Mind of the Moralist* and Juliet Mitchell's *Psychoanalysis and Feminism*) are, as a rule, uncomprehending, naïve, off the point, and biassed. Freud was wrong to say that no one who hasn't been analyzed has the "right" to discuss psychoanalysis—you just can't say that—but he was correct in believing that people who have had personal experience of psychoanalysis are in a better position to grasp psychoanalytic theory than those who have not. This could be said of any other discipline: to do it is to gain an understanding of it that can be gained in no other way. The critics of psychoanalysis argue that people who have been analyzed are "brainwashed" into "believing in" psychoanalysis. But the same could be said of people who have come to a sympathetic understanding of Beethoven's genius through learning to play his piano sonatas.

There are people who play Beethoven and are left cold by him; and there are people who have been analyzed—and even people who are analysts—who remain impervious to

Freud's theory of the mind. From the beginning of psychoanalysis to the present—from Adler, Jung, Rank, and Stekel
to Fromm, Sullivan, Horney, Alexander, and, possibly, Kohut—there have been people within psychoanalysis to whom
psychoanalysis was never really congenial. After sojourning
for a while in the chilly castle of psychoanalysis, they pass on
to smaller, cozier habitations. The present-day proponents of
the seduction theory are new versions of those old revisionists.
They are people in whom the germ of psychoanalytic thought
has never caught hold. Masson's repudiation of psychoanalysis is hardly a new story to students of defections from the
fold; nor is the idea that Anna Freud and Kurt Eissler were
"taken in" by Masson a startling one. Here, too, there is a
venerable precedent. It has become a kind of cliché about
Freud that he was "no *Menschenkenner*." Throughout his
life, he was beset (as who of us isn't?) by the affliction of
overestimation. Breuer, Fliess, and Jung were the most prominent of those who came within the orbit of Freud's propen-
sity for idealization followed by disillusionment. The story
of Eissler and Anna Freud and Masson, like the story of
Freud and Fliess/Breuer/Jung, is a cautionary tale whose
moral seems so obvious that there may be another, more
subtle one hidden behind it.

3

AT Chez Panisse, the maître d'hôtel came to tell us that our
table was ready, and after we had ordered from the
interesting menu (the restaurant is itself a member of a revisionist movement: the reaction, known as *la nouvelle cui-*

sine, against French culinary orthodoxy), Masson told me with relish about how he had won the confidence of Anna Freud. "I had been corresponding with her since the early seventies, and I had met her a few times, but it wasn't until 1977 that she began to show any real interest in me. I did something then that really impressed her. I had asked her if I could see the Freud-Fliess letters of 1897, figuring that she'd tell me to get lost, and she told me to get lost. Then I said, 'I'd like to see just *one* letter from that year,' and she said O.K., and gave me permission to see that one letter. And I found a *major error* that Jones had made in his biography. He said that Freud wrote to Fliess about Breuer that he 'was glad he saw no more of him; the very sight would make him inclined to emigrate.' I discovered that what Freud had really written was 'How fortunate that I no longer see Breuer. He would have surely advised me to emigrate.' When I pointed out this mistranslation to Anna Freud, she was very impressed. I had asked for that particular letter because while reading Jones I had had the feeling that something was wrong—it just hadn't sounded right. But finding the error was a piece of incredible luck. Although Jones made many errors, this happened to be the biggest error he ever made. I never found another of its magnitude. And Anna Freud was quite dazzled. It was like magic—'Masson says there's something wrong, I show him an unpublished letter, and he uncovers a serious error. This guy is good.' So when I asked her again for the 1897 letters, this time she said yes— of course, after consulting with Eissler. Then, a year later, in 1978, I asked Anna Freud for permission to publish a complete edition of the Freud-Fliess correspondence. At first, she was reluctant, but finally she said, 'Yes, I have yielded to Dr. Eissler's arguments, and I give my permission for a complete edition, since people want it so much.' But then she said to me, 'How can you do this work? You don't know enough German.' I said, 'I'll go to Germany and learn it in six months.' She said, 'You can't learn German that fast.' In the fall of 1979, I went to Munich, and six months later I came back speaking fluent German."

Masson paused to take a few appreciative bites of his baked goat-cheese appetizer, and then explained that he had gone to Germany without his family. (A daughter, Simone, was born in 1974.) "Terri and I were having problems, and I thought it would be a good idea for me to be away for a year." The Massons had moved from Toronto to Berkeley the previous year. He had been offered a visiting professorship in Sanskrit at the University of California at Berkeley, and on graduating from the Toronto Institute of Psychoanalysis he decided to ask for a sabbatical from the University of Toronto, take up the visiting professorship, and then start analytic practice in a place whose physical and professional climate was more congenial to him than that of Toronto; once established as an analyst in Berkeley, he would resign from his Toronto post. In Toronto, at both the university and the institute, Masson had had almost nothing but trouble. At the university, he had challenged the autocratic policies of the head of his department, with the result that when a new dean came in and surveyed the chaos he could think of nothing else to do but abolish the Sanskrit department in its entirety. At the institute, Masson had challenged his teachers and his training analyst, and was graduated, he says, "only so that they could finally get rid of me." In the opinion of colleagues at the University of Toronto (and of the abolishing dean), Masson was justified in his fight against the authoritarian head Sanskritist. And from the institute there also comes some corroboration of Masson's view of himself as a troublemaker who had good reason for making trouble. Of his five-year analysis Masson says that the only thing he got out of it was an object lesson in how not to treat his own patients. But the patients never materialized. The San Francisco senior analysts who had been so taken with Masson at congresses were evidently not sufficiently taken to be willing to refer patients to him. "To analysts, I was a private asset and a public liability. I had a total of three patients in Berkeley, and one of them came through Eissler," Masson said bitterly. "I realized that this wasn't going to work. I wasn't going to be able to practice analysis. So going to Germany was a kind of solution to that problem, too."

While in Munich, Masson received frequent letters from Eissler, and on April 17, 1980, Eissler wrote him a letter that was to change the lives of both men. "I was driving back from a weekend in Ischia with a girlfriend, and we were exchanging fantasies about what would be awaiting us when we got back to Munich," Masson told me. "What would make us happy? And I said that what would make me happiest would be to find a letter for me from Kurt Eissler saying 'Dear Professor Masson'—he called me that even though we were very close and I had begged him to call me Jeff—'Dear Professor Masson, you should take over the Archives from me.' And, I swear, there waiting for me was a letter from Eissler that said, 'I am haunted by a fantasy that you should take over the Archives. You have the idealism, know-how, enthusiasm, scholarship, honesty—briefly, all the qualities necessary.'"

As I later realized, when I read Eissler's letter itself, Masson was quoting Eissler's actual words from memory.

The letter continued, "I dream of an endowment fund of $400,000, which would give you $40,000 annually. Would that be enough? You would be salaried Secretary. I am selfish: I want to get rid of all that. I have postponed writing what I really want to write about for years, and it is high time that I turn to my own interests, but the Sigmund Freud Foundation and the Sigmund Freud Archives have become quite a bother. This is strictly confidential, and is not to be repeated even to Mrs. Masson. . . ."

Masson wrote back a long, ecstatic letter:

I can't think of anything better than to be on a salary and to be the Secretary of the Archives. The sum you mention is very reasonable. That is slightly more than I now get from Toronto. But even if nothing happened in the way of salary, I would be more than happy—it is my dream—to become the Secretary of the Archives.

I have had to recognize that I am not the best material for a practicing analyst. I am not patient enough, not quiet enough, not modest enough. Also, I love to discover, uncover, probe the past, find out the truth. At that I am superb, and patients love it. I really set to work with vigor and pleasure. But when it comes to the "working through," I am really no good. Then I feel like sending them to some quiet woman analyst who can listen in peace. So I know I should not practice.

I should be doing research; it is the one thing I am really good at. I kept asking myself: How can it ever be possible for you to do what you do best? It seemed so unlikely. I pictured, with mounting sadness, a life in Toronto teaching Sanskrit and eventually being forced to accept some position (there was some talk of my being offered the chair at Harvard) that would force me to do only that. And I really don't enjoy it anymore. It strikes me as too trivial, too far removed from the real concerns of a person.

Nothing, therefore, could be more suited to me than the Archives—and I would be paid for it on top of that! It is a real dream, an absolutely ideal life. I could not ask for more.

It still feels unreal. Can it really be? Is this really happening? I am deeply grateful for everything you have already done (I really owe my career to you) for me, and I will harbor no resentment if you tell me to forget this fantasy, even though it was a mutual one.

A few weeks later, Masson returned to Berkeley via New York, where he called on Eissler. "We had a long, emotional meeting for two days," Masson told me. Eissler had meant it. "He showed me this big black notebook that contained information about every letter: how much he had paid for it, where he had got it, when it could be published, whether it could be seen—all that sort of thing," Masson continued. " 'It's all yours,' he told me. 'All these things I have here, they're yours. I am old and tired, and I want to spend the last years of my life doing other things.' It was very moving. Then Eissler got Muriel Gardiner—a lovely and remarkable woman, a psychoanalyst who was in the underground in Austria before the war and saved a lot of Jews, and who has a fabulous amount of money—to donate funds for my salary through her New-Land Foundation, and in the fall of 1980 I was appointed Projects Director by the Board of the Archives, with a salary of thirty thousand dollars a year. The next November, I was to succeed Eissler as Secretary, and then, when Anna Freud died, I was to be the director of a Freud museum, to be established in Anna Freud's house at 20 Maresfield Gardens, in Hampstead—Muriel Gardiner had bought the house from Anna Freud and given it to the Archives. When the news of Anna Freud's death came, I was to get on the next plane to London and immediately take all the letters in the house to the American Embassy and then to the Library of Congress. Eissler was afraid that relatives would come in and take the letters—a letter signed by Freud is worth two thousand dollars today, and there were thousands of Freud's letters in the house. It was a beautiful house, but it was dark and sombre and dead. Nothing ever went on there. I was the only person who ever came. I would have renovated it, opened it up, brought it to life. Maresfield Gardens would have been a center of scholarship, but it would also have been a place of sex, women, fun. It would have been like the change in *The Wizard of Oz,* from black-and-white into color.

"When word got around that Eissler had made me his successor, other things started to come my way. I was made a director of the Freud Copyrights. This is the group, made up of Mark Paterson, Masud Khan, Mrs. E. L. Freud, and me— I still haven't been kicked off it, for some reason—that controls the copyright on Freud's writings. My appointment happened through Masud Khan. He's a well-known English analyst. At first, he was very suspicious of me, but when he saw the future—how I was coming in and taking over from Eissler—he wanted to be on good terms. So he invited me to his house and wrapped his arms around me and said, 'My dear boy, you must become a director of the Copyrights.' He's a very handsome man, about six feet seven. His full title is Prince Masud Khan—he's an Indian raja—and he's very fashionable. He used to be married to a Russian prima ballerina. And he's generous—he gave me books and a big picture of himself at our first meeting—and very articulate. He says what he thinks. He's got class and he's fun, and we took to each other right away. Now, of course, he doesn't speak to me. He was the one who said that I must be kept out of Anna Freud's funeral.

"Then the Harvard University Press jumped on the bandwagon and made me general editor of a new series of Freud's letters—to his boyhood friend Eduard Silberstein, to his colleagues Abraham and Ferenczi, to his friend Ludwig Binswanger—which they would publish in a uniform edition, along with the Freud-Fliess letters. If I had been somebody off the street and had called Arthur Rosenthal, the director of the Harvard Press, he wouldn't have talked to me. But as Projects Director of the Freud Archives and a director of the Freud Copyrights I was someone to conjure with.

"And then, finally, Anna Freud gave me access to the formidable cupboard. This was a huge, dark wooden cupboard that stood on the landing outside her bedroom and was filled with about a thousand letters from Freud. No one had ever read them. I had heard about this cupboard from Eissler, who had once gone through it with Anna Freud, but very quickly, so he hadn't had a chance to look at things. I asked Anna Freud if I could see the letters, and she asked Eissler, and he said, 'Yes, he may,' and so I started going through the cupboard. It was a treasure trove! There were all kinds of things in it that no one knew about: letters between Freud and Charcot, a letter from Fliess to Freud, hundreds of letters from Freud to Minna Bernays, family letters. It was the last bastion. No one else had ever had access to the cupboard.

"It all looked ideal. I was young, dynamic, enthusiastic,

and scholarly, not committed to any faction within psycho-analysis but simply interested in Freud. I didn't really care about money, I liked to travel, I knew everybody, I could get things going. They needed someone my age. All these guys are old. They needed someone who would be around for a while. Eissler couldn't get over his luck in finding me. I was like his son.

"Of course, many people were offended by my manner. They found me arrogant, brash, impatient, intolerant, too critical, too Jewish. They would complain about me to Eissler. He would tell me, 'You don't know the number of telephone calls I get about you! Every time you go anywhere on a trip, I get letters and calls saying, "Leash your maniac Masson. You don't know what you've let loose on the analytic world. He's going through everybody's papers, he's digging up all kinds of things, he's talking about it, he's irrepressible. This is not good for psychoanalysis."' And Eissler would say, 'I've protected you against everybody.' He and Anna Freud and Muriel Gardiner were my three friends in analysis, and they happened to be so powerful that my enemies paled into in-significance. But almost everyone else in the analytic world would have done anything to get rid of me. They were envious of me, but I think they also genuinely felt that I was a mistake and a nuisance and a potential danger to psycho-analysis—a really critical danger. They sensed that I could single-handedly bring down the whole business—and, let's face it, there's a lot of money in that business. And they were right to be frightened, because what I was discovering was dynamite."

I asked Masson what this dynamite was. What had he found in Anna Freud's house that was so damaging to psy-choanalysis and cast such a bad light on Freud's character?

Masson swallowed a few mouthfuls of the striped bass with fennel that had been lying untouched on his plate, and replied, "It's quite complicated, and I'm not sure where to begin. Maybe the best thing would be for you to first read some things I've written—the Yale paper and a paper on nineteenth-century psychiatry—and some things by other writers, and then the whole story will make more sense to you. I'll drop the stuff off at your hotel later today."

The conversation turned to Masson's shift from Sanskrit to psychoanalysis, and I asked him how he had become involved with analysis.

"It started at Harvard in the sixties," he said. "When I first went there as an undergraduate, I was an obnoxious person. I knew nothing. The only things I could do were read and sleep with women. I had come from a school in Uruguay. The reason I came from a school in Uruguay was that in 1958 this Indian guru who was living with my family —he was actually an English Jew named Paul Brunton, who wrote books on Indian mysticism—told my parents that he had received secret information that the Third World War was coming within three months, and that we should escape to South America. We were then living in Switzerland. My father is a gem merchant who doesn't like to stay in any one place too long. His father was a gem merchant, too—a Bessarabian gem merchant, named Moussaieff, who went to Paris in the twenties and adopted the name Masson. My parents named me Jeffrey Lloyd Masson, but in 1975 I decided to change my middle name to Moussaieff—it sounded better. We had moved all through my childhood—from Chicago, where I was born, to L.A. to Arizona to Hawaii and back to L.A., and then to Switzerland—so moving to South America wasn't such a big deal. But then the Third

World War didn't come, and I was nineteen and didn't want
to spend the rest of my life at the University of Montevideo,
so I applied to Yale, Harvard, Princeton, and Stanford and
got into all of them, I don't know why—by mistake, probably, because I hadn't been all that bright as a high-school student. I went to Harvard because another guru living with us,
named John Levy—Brunton was my father's guru and Levy
was my mother's—told my parents that it would be good for
my character if I was sent to the least pleasant and friendly
of the colleges I had visited, and Harvard was that. When I
got there, the first thing I did was to persuade them to make
me a sophomore. I shouldn't have even been a freshman!
But for some reason they agreed to make me a sophomore.
Then I decided that it was beneath me to live in the dorms,
so I talked my way into a three-room apartment in a place
called the Center for the Study of World Religions, where
visiting professors and graduate students lived. I was unbearable. But Harvard was unbearable, too. It was such a snobbish place then. There were two students who were particularly unpleasant to me—Wendy O'Flaherty and Richard
Gombrich. They were also in Sanskrit, and they were very
wise and snobbish, and were always doing things with Daniel
Ingalls, the chairman of the Sanskrit department. Gombrich,
who is the son of the famous English art historian Ernst
Gombrich, was very sharp and witty, and he liked to use me
as the butt of jokes. He hates me to this day. He recently
wrote a really nasty review of my book *The Oceanic Feeling*
for the *Journal of the Royal Asiatic Society*. [Masson later
showed me the review, which began, "Rarely—mercifully
rarely—it happens that one is sent a book for review which
is so bad that truth cannot be reconciled with charity or
honesty with politeness."] Wendy was even worse, in her

37

way, though I thought, Well, at least she's a woman. I remember once trying to touch her, and she looked at me and said, 'Frankly, I don't think you're man enough to have an affair with me.' I ran into this sort of thing everywhere I went at Harvard. Then I met a rather attractive older graduate student, and I had an affair with her. One day, she took me to some art event, and she was sorry afterward. She said, 'Well, it's very nice sleeping with you in your room, but you're the kind of person who should never leave the room—you're just a social embarrassment anywhere else, though you do fine in your own room.' And, you know, in their way, if not in so many words, Eissler and Anna Freud told me the same thing. They liked me well enough 'in my own room.' They loved to hear from me what creeps and dolts analysts are. I was like an intellectual gigolo—you get your pleasure from him, but you don't take him out in public. Do you know what Anna Freud once said to me? She said, 'If my father were alive today, he would not become an analyst.' I swear, those were her words. No, wait. This is important. *I* said that to *her*. I said, 'Miss Freud, I have the feeling that if your father were alive today he would not become an analyst,' and she said, 'You are right.'

"Erik Erikson was teaching at Harvard when I was there, and I went to him and asked if I could go into treatment with him. My main symptom was total promiscuity—sleeping with every woman I could meet. He said no, but he sent me to someone he said he had great respect for, and I was in therapy with this man for a few years. But eight years later, when I was teaching in Toronto, I still had the symptom, so I went into therapy again, and then into five-times-a-week analysis. The trouble never seemed to get any better, and I figured it must have something to do with my childhood. I didn't say to myself, 'Well, you're just a lovable guy—you just love women, and women just love you.' I knew there was something wrong. I'd slept with close to a thousand women by the time I got to Toronto. And I'd fallen in love about five times. Not a great number. And even when I was in love with a woman it didn't stop me from sleeping with other women. So I realized there was something to look for. And when I went into therapy there were things about it that just fascinated me. The idea that there could be feelings that you're not aware of utterly fascinated me. The idea of counter-phobia fascinated me: that you could climb mountains because you were terrified of heights, that you would seek out dangers because the dangers held such fear for you. The importance of dreams: that there are feelings you can recover in dreams that you've never had in real life; that you can discover from a dream that you're in love with someone. The idea of repressed memories, of early memories—all these analytic ideas captivated me, and the more I read the more fascinated I became, and the more I read Freud the more admiring I became. But I was not doing anything historical then.

"After getting my Ph.D. in Sanskrit from Harvard, and spending a few years in India, I got my first job, as assistant professor of Sanskrit at the University of Toronto. And as soon as I got there—the first day I taught Sanskrit—I had one of those awakenings that people sometimes have. I realized that this was not for me—that I couldn't do this for the rest of my life. I couldn't sit here with four students, all eccentric, and read this little script. I just couldn't. I was bored out of my mind. I was twenty-nine years old, and I had a Ph.D. from Harvard, and I didn't know what to do with my life. I knew I couldn't go on. Finally, I met a very lovely guy by the name of Charles Hanly—a professor of philosophy who was in training at the Toronto Institute of Psychoanalysis—and he said, 'Why don't you train as an analyst?' and that was how I got into psychoanalysis.

"When I first arrived in Toronto, I had total admiration for anybody who was a psychiatrist or an analyst. I was very naïve. I was very young for my age. My fantasy was that all psychiatrists and analysts are fascinating people. I would go over to the university's psychiatric hospital—which I now consider one of the rat holes of the world but then thought was the most wonderful place in the world—and I would hang around the classes in the hope of meeting some students of psychiatry. And then when I got into the world of analysis it was utterly fascinating to me. For many years, I would associate only with analysts. I went out to dinner every night with analysts, partied with analysts, refused to see anyone who wasn't an analyst. Terri—whom I had met and married by this time—was appalled by this. She'd say, 'But, Jeff, they're so dull.' And I'd say, 'Ah, yes. But that's only because I'm a candidate. They don't want to say anything to me. When I become an analyst, they'll change.' It was a total delusion. It was part of the transference. When you're in analysis, analysts are fascinating. My classmates at the institute used to take their cars and drive to their analysts' houses and hide in the shrubbery and watch their wives and kids. It's a very strange state of mind. At first, I was utterly enraptured by my analyst, Dr. V. He was very sarcastic, very funny and witty, a great mimic. I had a lot of fun with him, and he with me. He'd say, 'I'm glad you come at the end of my day, Masson. You really cheer me up. I look forward to this hour all day. At last, I can have a bit of fun.' He was wrong to tell me that, but I just lapped it up. I just loved it. I'd say, 'It's not like seeing E., right?' E. was one of my classmates. And Dr. V. would say, 'That's right, E. is Dullsville, Masson. Between you and me, he's Dullsville.' E. *was* Dullsville—but that my analyst would make such a confession to me! It wasn't analysis, but it was great fun. But then Dr. V. started going after me. He would scream at me and threaten me, and it stopped being fun. One day, I'd had enough, and I said, 'Dr. V., I'm leaving. I'm not going to take this anymore. I'm going to have a consultation with another analyst.' And Dr. V. said, 'You do that. But you understand, of course, that it's your word against mine. And who do you think they're going to believe, Masson, when I tell them you're a raving lunatic and should be dropped from the analytic institute immediately?' He scared the hell out of me. At first, when Dr. V. screamed at me I'd think, He's right. It's the only way to get through to me. I'm a hard nut to crack, and he's doing it out of compassion. He's doing it because he really cares. He's trying to help me. You know how the transference is. I made a million excuses for him. It wasn't until he threatened me that I realized that this man could harm me.

"Once, after the analysis was over, I went to Dr. V.'s house for lunch, and I thought, There he is—just this ordinary little guy. Then, a few weeks later, I met him at the institute, and we were having this talk in his office about the transference and how it affects one's perception of physical appearance, and I said to him, 'You know, I always thought of you as an immense man, and it came as a great shock to me the other day when you stood up and I realized that I was practically a head taller than you.' And he said, 'What are you talking about?' And I said, 'Well, just the fact that I'm taller than you.' And he said, '*You* taller than *me*? You're out of your mind!' And I said, 'Dr. V., I *am* taller than you, I assure you.' And he said, 'Stand up,' and I stood up, and he stood up, and I towered over him, and he looked me in the eye—from a good four inches beneath me—and said, '*Now* are you convinced that I'm taller than you?' So to be polite I said, 'Yes, I see.' But I thought, This guy is out of his mind.

"Actually, analysts are all terribly dull people. I've never met an analyst who wasn't ultimately dull, and I'm sure if I had met Freud I would have found him dull, too, after a while. I don't think he was that interesting, ultimately. But I didn't know that then. I was utterly fascinated by psychoanalysts and psychoanalysis, and I had a compulsive habit of reading psychoanalytic papers. I would take something like *The Psychoanalytic Quarterly,* and I'd begin with the year one, and I'd read through it, issue by issue, to the last issue—just read through it, every single article, as if I were searching for something. I read literally thousands and thousands of articles that I now consider total junk and regret having read. I'd draw up lists of what I thought were the good articles, and make Xeroxes of them. At home, I have about four thousand reprints—box after box of Xeroxes of articles that I thought were significant.

"Whenever I actually got to know an analyst, disappointment would set in. They didn't seem to be really interested in psychoanalysis. They would say things like 'Well, we don't read Freud anymore, he's passé,' and I'd think, God, that's weird. But then I'd tell myself, 'Well, that's Toronto; it's really a backwater. When I get to the real heart of things, it will all be different.' And I formed this fantasy of how in every city there is this inner core of four or five tough old analysts—all, appropriately enough, the age of my father— who aren't frightened of anything, who tell the truth: Sam Lipton, Brian Bird, Vic Calef, Ed Weinshel, Eissler at the very pinnacle, and, finally, Anna Freud. These are the people who would be undaunted by everything, and who would love my work. And it was true: as long as I was publishing things that were not really historical—that were very admiring of Freud and very critical of everyone else—they *did* love my work. As long as I was doing that kind of thing, I was the darling of the International Psycho-Analytical Association. I gave four papers at International meetings, one after another, which is unheard of for a student. And I thought, Great! There *is* this world outside of Toronto where people are really interested in the truth. But the closer I got to the person of Freud, and the closer I got to the real history of what had gone on, the more my so-called friends retreated from me, and I realized that it wasn't me but the evidence I was turning up. Finally, even Eissler got frightened, and felt that he had to dump me."

The lunch crowd at Chez Panisse was thinning out. Masson looked at his watch and said he had to pick up Simone from school. He and Terri had amicably split up and were sharing the custody of the child; for the moment Simone was living with him, he said. We made a date for lunch the next day—which would give him the morning with Alice Miller and me the time to do the required reading for an understanding of his ominous findings.

4

I N THE large packet of papers that Masson left at my hotel, one item stood out from the rest in its shock value. It was a quiet, restrained, and devastating forty-page paper, written not by Masson but by, of all people, the late Max Schur, who had been Freud's personal physician during his final years in Vienna and London and had then emigrated to New York, where he took up psychoanalysis. Schur's paper, published in 1966 in an obscure volume called *Psychoanalysis—A General Psychology,* and innocuously entitled "Some Additional 'Day Residues' of 'The Specimen Dream of Psychoanalysis,' " tells the horrifying story of a patient of Freud's named Emma Eckstein, who had come to him in 1894 with hysterical symptoms, and to whom he had indirectly caused severe and near-fatal injury. The story emerges from ten unpublished letters of Freud to Fliess, which Schur had come across while reading the complete Freud-Fliess correspondence. (Anna Freud had given him special permission to study it for a biography of Freud he was writing.)

The "specimen dream" appears in Freud's *The Interpretation of Dreams* (1900) as an example of how a dream may be taken apart and analyzed; it evidently was the first dream (dreamed by Freud on the night of July 23–24, 1895) that he thus anatomized and interpreted. It is a dream of guilt and self-exoneration. The wish at its center (according to Freudian theory, every dream is a wish-fulfillment dream) is Freud's wish to get himself off the hook in regard to a patient—not Emma but a later patient pseudonymously named Irma—whom he is not sure he has done well by, and, at the same time, to put the blame on several of his colleagues. "Day residues" is the term Freud used to signify the events of the day or days preceding a dream which are its *données;* Schur stretches the meaning of the term to include events that happened weeks, or even months, before the dream was dreamed. He argues that Freud did not go far enough in his dream analysis, and that beyond Irma there lies Emma, whom Freud had begun to treat, or mistreat, the previous winter. It was Freud's practice at that time to send his hysterical patients to his friend Fliess for consultations, to determine whether their trouble wasn't, after all, physical rather than mental—specifically, whether it wasn't *nasal.* Fliess had developed a bizarre theory of the nasal origin of various gastro-intestinal, neurological, and (above all) sexual disorders, which he treated by the application of cocaine to the nasal membranes and/or by surgery on the turbinate bone and the nasal sinuses. If one finds it hard to believe that Freud should have endorsed such an obviously crackpot theory and quackish therapy, one should remember that to his contemporaries Freud's own theories seemed equally lunatic, and his therapy equally disreputable. Freud's use of Fliess as a confidant and a source of emotional and intellectual solace has been likened to the use that a patient makes of his analyst—with the important distinction, however, that since Freud wasn't paying Fliess money for listening to him, he had to pay in the currency of reciprocal sympathy and support.

Freud had sent Irma to Fliess for an examination to see whether her gastric pains might be of nasal origin, and the examination evidently had been negative, since no mention is made of any nasal treatment for Irma. Emma was less fortunate. After being examined by Fliess, who had come from Berlin to Vienna at Freud's request for this purpose, Emma underwent nasal surgery by Fliess. A few days later,

Fliess returned to Berlin, and then the trouble started. Emma began to suffer intense pain, swelling, and bleeding; a foetid odor came from the cavity. On March 4, 1895, Freud wrote to Fliess, briefly and helplessly telling him of these developments. Then, on March 8, Freud broke the following horrendous news to Fliess:

> I wrote you that the swelling and bleeding wouldn't let up, and that suddenly a foetid odor set in along with an obstacle to irrigation. . . . I arranged for Gersuny [a prominent Viennese surgeon] to be called in, and he inserted a drain, hoping that things would work out if discharge were reëstablished. Otherwise he behaved in a rather rejecting way. Two days later, I was awakened early in the morning— quite profuse bleeding had started again, with pain, etc. I got a telephone message from Gersuny that he could come only in the evening, so I asked R. [an ear-nose-and-throat specialist] to meet me at Miss Emma's apartment. This we did at noon. There was moderate bleeding from the nose and mouth; the foetid odor was very bad. R. cleaned the area surrounding the opening, removed some blood clots which were sticking to the surface, and suddenly pulled at something like a thread. He kept right on pulling, and before either of us had time to think, at least half a meter of gauze had been removed from the cavity. The next moment came a flood of blood. The patient turned white, her eyes bulged, and her pulse was no longer palpable. However, immediately after this he packed the cavity with fresh iodoform gauze, and the hemorrhage stopped. It had lasted about half a minute, but this was enough to make the poor creature, who by then we had lying quite flat, unrecognizable. In the meantime, or actually afterwards, something else happened. At the moment the foreign

body came out, and everything had become obvious to me, immediately after which I was confronted with the sight of the patient, I felt sick. After she had been packed, I fled to the next room, drank a bottle of water, and felt rather miserable. The brave Frau Doktor then brought me a small glass of cognac, and I felt like myself again.

R. remained with the patient until I arranged to have both of them taken to the Loew Sanatorium by S. Nothing more happened that evening. The following day, i.e. yesterday, Thursday, the operation was repeated with the assistance of Gersuny. The bone was broken wide open, the packing removed, and the wound curetted. There was hardly any further bleeding. She had not lost consciousness during the severe hemorrhage scene, and when I returned to the room somewhat shaky, she greeted me with the condescending remark: "This is the strong sex."

I don't think I had been overwhelmed by the blood; affects were welling up in me at that moment. So we had done her an injustice. She had not been abnormal at all, but a piece of iodoform gauze had gotten torn off when you removed the rest, and stayed in for fourteen days, interfering with the healing process, after which it had torn away and provoked the bleeding. The fact that this mishap should have happened to *you,* how you would react to it when you learned about it, what others would make of it, how wrong I had been to press you to operate in a foreign city, where you couldn't handle the aftercare, how my intention of getting the best for the poor girl was insidiously thwarted, with the resultant danger to her life—all this came over me simultaneously. . . .

The tearing off of the iodoform gauze was one of those accidents that happen to the most fortunate and cautious of surgeons. . . . Gersuny mentioned that he had had a similar experience, and that he therefore used

iodoform wicks instead of gauze. . . . Of course, no one
blames you in any way, nor do I know why they should.
And I only hope that you will come as quickly as I did
to feel only pity. Rest assured that I felt no need to
restore my trust in you. I only want to add that I hesitated for a day to tell you all about it, and that then I
began to be ashamed, and here is the letter.

That this, and all other letters pertaining to the Emma
episode, had been omitted from *The Origins of Psychoanalysis* is hard to justify from the point of view of scholarship but easy to understand from that of filial piety. Freud
does not shine in this story. He doesn't come out as badly as
Fliess does, of course, but in his eagerness to exonerate his
friend he betrays a callousness toward his patient that, for
once, causes the reader of Freud's letters to withhold some
of his sympathy. Freud's own dealings with Emma may well
have been exemplary—or as exemplary as they could be under
the circumstances—but his letters to Fliess about Emma are
lacking in the quality that caused Kurt Eissler to give his
review of a collection of Freud's letters the title "Mankind at
Its Best." When, after describing the ghastly scene of the
discovery of the gauze in Emma's nose, Freud can wring his
hands over "the fact that this mishap should have happened
to *you*" (italics Schur's and mine), the reader scarcely knows
where to look.

Schur's own idea in publishing Freud's letters about the
Emma episode was not to show Freud in a poor light but,
rather, to illustrate the power of the transference in his relationship to Fliess. It was Freud's urgent need to believe in
Fliess, to think of him as infallible, that blinded him to
reality and prevented him from seeing how badly Fliess

had botched the case. As time went on (and poor Emma was finally out of danger), Freud progressively downgraded Fliess's culpability, and finally was able to persuade himself that it was *Emma herself,* and not Fliess, who had been at fault. In a letter of April 16, 1896, Freud promises Fliess that he will soon tell him of "a quite surprising explanation of Emma's hemorrhages, which will give you great satisfaction," and on April 26 he writes, "You were right; her hemorrhages were hysterical, brought on by *longing.*" Emma, who had (inexplicably) gone back into treatment with Freud, had revealed to him that she had a long history of hysterical nosebleeding. In a letter of May 4, Freud happily tells Fliess of Emma's confession that in the sanatorium, after the incident of the removal of the gauze, "she began to feel restless out of unconscious longing and the intention of drawing me to her side." He continues, "And since I did not come during the night, she renewed the hemorrhage as an unfailing means of reawakening my affection. She bled spontaneously three times, and each hemorrhage lasted approximately four days, which must be significant." Schur dryly comments, "Nowadays, we would of course expect a careful hematological work-up to establish what kind of 'bleeder' Emma was. But in this letter Freud was—without mentioning it—continuing with the exculpation of Fliess! The iodoform gauze was buried and forgotten!"

Schur cites a few more references to Emma (in letters of 1897), in which Freud tells Fliess of sadistic, blood-ridden, and evidently imaginary "scenes" that Emma recounted in her analysis. "It would therefore seem that Emma was one of the first patients who offered Freud a clue to the crucial realization that what his patients had described to him as actual seduction episodes were fantasies," Schur notes. He does not push the point. He hovers near, but does not alight on, the possible connection between Freud's wish to believe that Fliess's horrendous error had never happened (or, at any rate, had had no consequences) and his repudiation of a theory that traced hysteria to actual body- and soul-damaging events in favor of one emphasizing the power of fantasy.

The connection that Schur skirted was the one that Masson pounced on and held up as conclusive evidence of Freud's intellectual shabbiness. When I met with Masson the next day, he declared, with characteristic hyperbole, "In my opinion, Emma Eckstein is the single most important person in the history of psychoanalysis. She was the first victim of psychoanalysis, and one of the great heroines of twentieth-century thought. Her story is the wedge that is going to topple psychoanalysis. When analysts read my book *The Assault on Truth,* in which Emma will loom very large, they will ask for my neck, I assure you. They will say, 'He was bad enough at Yale, he was worse in those articles in the *Times,* and now he's utterly impossible. The man must be murdered.' I won't be surprised if the analytic mafia puts out a contract on me." He laughed gleefully, and went on, "Freud abandoned the seduction theory because he couldn't face the truth about what Fliess had done to Emma. He needed to believe that Fliess was innocent and Emma was guilty. So he developed the theory that all patients lie—they they are made sick by their fantasies, and not by anything real that has happened to them. He gave up a very powerful theory for a lesser one in order to exculpate his friend. He did it unconsciously, of course, and he did it for other reasons as well—I went into some of those in my Yale lecture—but he did it, and ever since then analysts have been denying the realities of their patients' lives. When Freud abandoned the seduction theory, it was the death of psychoanalysis. The received truth is that it was the *birth* of psychoanalysis, but it wasn't; it was the end, and, deep down, all analysts know it was the end. That is why they all feel like such frauds. They do analysis because it's good business, but in their innermost souls they feel utterly fraudulent. If I sat down with any analyst for a few days and grilled him and really pushed him, he would admit that he doesn't like what he's doing, that he doesn't believe in it, that in some deep sense he feels dishonest. I know that's how they all feel. I know that even Freud himself felt like that after he abandoned the seduction theory."

Masson then told me the curious prehistory of his obsessive interest in the seduction theory. Robert Fliess, one of the two sons of Wilhelm, became a psychoanalyst in Berlin in the thirties and later emigrated to New York, where he served as a training analyst at the New York Psychoanalytic Institute and pursued a long, distinguished career as an analyst and teacher. But toward the end of his life he became seriously disturbed, and formed the idea—which even Masson concedes is crazy—that every single one of his patients (and, indeed, all neurotic patients of all analysts) had been sexually abused by one parent or the other. (Fliess characterized such parents as "ambulatory psychotics.") He put this extreme notion into his book *Symbol, Dream, and Psychosis,* written a year before his death, in 1970, along with the idea that Freud's repudiation of the seduction theory was the end of his "honeymoon with truth." *"No one is ever made sick by his fantasies,"* Fliess wrote, and added, "Only traumatic memories in repression can cause the neurosis. This fact alone is sufficient reason for discounting Freud's later 'denial.'" Masson went on, "Reading Fliess in the early seventies had a tremendous impact on me. He really influenced me. He was paranoid, and he went too far in saying that all patients were seduced, but he was right in saying that neurosis is always caused by something real. There is reason to think that Robert Fliess himself was seduced by his father. He hints at it in *Symbol, Dream, and Psychosis.*' "

Masson continued, "When I was in France last month, somebody said to me, 'Masson, leave America and come here. You're a celebrity, you'll have a full practice in twelve hours, everybody will go to you. You're the new Lacan. Charge anything you want, because Paris is very modish and you are *à la mode.*' But I won't do that. I can't. Because I don't believe in psychoanalysis any longer. I suppose that in a little while I will resign from the International Psycho-Analytical Association, though I think I'll wait until I can get the most effect out of it. Or wait until they try to throw me out, which shouldn't be long now, except that they'd be frightened of the publicity." Masson suddenly looked at his watch, broke off his monologue, and asked—we were sitting in my room at the Claremont—if he could use the phone. "I have to call Alice Miller," he explained, and sighed. "Do you remember I said I would set up a meeting for her in that guy Goldstine's mansion? Well, now she's found out that he's a sex therapist, and she's not sure she wants the meeting. She says it might be bad for her reputation to be mixed up with people like that. She said she would think it over and let me know what she's decided. I said I would call her at twelve-thirty." Masson dialled, spoke briefly with Alice Miller, and hung up with another sigh. "Oy," he said. "She's decided she doesn't want the meeting. What am I going to tell Goldstine? It's so embarrassing. He's bought twelve copies of her book to distribute. He's invited people. What a pain this is. May I use your phone again?" Masson dialled again and apologetically informed Goldstine of Alice Miller's change of heart. The conversation was brief; the sex therapist evidently took the news calmly.

While Masson spoke on the telephone, I pondered an incongruity that had struck me the night before while I was reading the paper he had delivered before the Western New England Psychoanalytic Society, in New Haven. In marked contrast to the extravagantly anti-psychoanalytic and anti-Freudian stand that Masson was now taking, the "Yale paper," as Masson likes to call it, even though the society has no connection with Yale, was respectful of psychoanalysis and of Freud, and its tone was scholarly and fairly quiet. Here and there in it, Masson would lapse into a kind of boyishness he is prone to, but on the whole the paper was as sober, and even, in places, as tedious, as the general run of psychoanalytic papers. The bulk of it was devoted to an extravagantly admiring discussion of Freud's 1896 paper on the seduction theory, "The Aetiology of Hysteria" (the paper is indeed one of Freud's most artfully argued essays), and to a pedantic and hard-to-follow argument regarding the possible influence of a certain Dr. Löwenfeld on Freud's decision to abandon the theory. When Masson hung up the telephone, I told him of these impressions, and asked him what had happened between the time of the lecture and the present to change him from a Freudian psychoanalyst with somewhat outré views into the bitter and belligerent anti-Freudian he had become.

Masson sidestepped my question. "You're right, there was nothing disrespectful of analysis in that paper," he said. "That remark about the sterility of psychoanalysis was some-

thing I tacked on at the last minute, and it was totally gra-
tuitous. I don't know why I put it in. The paper was very
scholarly, and I thought analysts would be fascinated by my
discoveries and would receive them with great warmth. But
something causes analysts to ignore my material and to focus
on me. Every time I give a paper, someone gets up and says,
'I'm not interested in that paper, I'm not interested in your
findings, I'm interested in you,' and then they come out with
some really cheap parlor analysis. 'I feel' (they said this when
I spoke in Chicago last year) 'that you are the Oedipal
child standing outside your parents' bedroom'—Freud and
Martha's, that is—'listening for the sounds of the primal
scene. That's what your research shows.' Listen, I don't need
cheap analysis. I got enough of that from my own analyst.
Just tell me what's wrong with my work—that's what I want
to hear. At Yale, after I gave the paper, there was a gathering
at the house of an older analyst named Richard Newman
and his wife, Lottie. (Lottie had been working with me on
the translation of the Freud-Fliess letters. She no longer
speaks to me.) About thirty analysts from the Western New
England Institute had come, and not one of them had the
guts or the brains to do anything but repeat the same old
tired psychoanalytic clichés. In some ways, it was like the
meeting where I was fired from the Archives. I was just as
alone. It was me against the thirty analysts. We sat in the
Newmans' big living room, and I said, 'Now, look, ladies and
gentlemen, do you really believe that there's no difference
between a fantasy and a reality?' And they said, 'Well, you
know, Freud has said it very clearly: there *is* no important
distinction to be made. In the end, it doesn't matter whether
it's fantasy or reality.' So I said, 'What do you do with something like Auschwitz? Surely you're not going to tell me that

the reality of Auschwitz doesn't matter—that all that matters is how people experience it? You're not going to tell me that there are different ways of experiencing Auschwitz, are you?' And they said, 'Yes, we are.' And then Sam Ritvo—a really decent, friendly, compassionate man—said, 'Let me tell you a story. I had a patient who came out of Auschwitz at the age of fifteen, and during his analysis he told me, "Auschwitz made a man of me." ' There was silence, and I thought everyone was going to be utterly appalled. I thought they would say that this was clearly a case of denial—that the patient talked that way because he couldn't face what had happened to him. But they didn't say that. They all agreed that Auschwitz had made a man of this patient. I felt like crying. I felt that this was not my environment. And most of them were Jews."

"I don't think they were arguing that Auschwitz was a good place," I said.

"No. But they were arguing that the experience of Auschwitz could have been a positive one for some people. They were saying that no one has the right to judge another person's experience—that you cannot say that everyone who was in Auschwitz came out badly damaged, which is what I would say. I believe that nobody came out of Auschwitz without being sick. I believe that that kind of trauma destroys people—it doesn't strengthen them. There are certain kinds of reality that are so overwhelming that they admit of only one interpretation. And if someone comes and says, 'Auschwitz made a man of me,' you know that that is a defense. The business of analysis is to undo that defense and get to the pain and the sorrow. But they were arguing that there is no such thing as reality—that there is no single Auschwitz. That is the worst thing that analysis has left the world: the notion that there is no reality, that there are only individual experiences of it. That is Freud's legacy to the twentieth century. He encouraged the whole twentieth century—anthropology, philosophy, sociology—to take that position, and it's a wrongheaded and dangerous position. And a very convenient one. It's what the Germans say: 'Auschwitz wasn't that bad. People were either sick before they came there or they weren't damaged. Auschwitz wouldn't have made a healthy person sick.' And that's an evil position. It upsets me so much. I find it so sad that an analyst should support the position that a child can be raped by her father and have a positive experience. It's an awful position."

"This sounds like a travesty of the analytic view."

"They've said it. There are hundreds of articles on that —on the positive effects of sexual seduction. There are classical articles that say it isn't always such a bad thing."

5

"OUR Western New England Institute in New Haven is not like the New York Psychoanalytic Institute," Elise Snyder, an analyst who had been at the gathering at the Newmans' told me. "It is very gentle and sweet up here. It's incredibly different from the New York group, which suffers from paranoia of a high degree. Here it's sort of *haimish,* and everyone was being very sweet to Masson; no one attacked him. But he behaved like an adolescent. It wasn't that he was being defensive—because no one was attacking him—but that he kept making more and more provocative and outrageous statements. He was like a bad boy throwing bags of water out the window and looking to see where they would burst. We all gradually became somewhat uneasy. People were talking about inner reality, the unconscious life, and at one point he turned to the group and said, quite angrily, 'Don't you care what really happened? Isn't that what is really important?' At which point the group just sort of backed off and the discussion ended. Because the answer to that, you know, from an analytic point of view is 'No, we're not so concerned with what really happened. We're concerned with how it got worked into the patient's inner life.' As Masson spoke, it began to be apparent that he didn't really understand psychoanalysis. I remember turning to someone and saying, 'He's not talking like an analyst. He's talking like someone who has read a lot of psychoanalytic writings but hasn't grasped what psychoanalysis is about.' So everybody kept backing farther and farther off, because this was not a scientific meeting but a social gathering. Everybody is terribly interested in those papers that Eissler won't let anybody see, and all of us there wanted to get a sense of Masson, because Eissler has been so impossible with regard to these papers—as Anna Freud was —and here was the person who was going to be sitting on them for the next twenty years. I came out of the Newmans' thinking, This man is a mistake."

6

AT NO time during our acquaintance did Masson answer my question about what had brought on his sudden virulent anti-Freudianism. As I came to realize, it was not the right question—as is probably the case with all un-answered (unanswerable) questions. Like the apostasy of Jung and Adler and the other "half-analysts" (as Freud called them), the apostasy of Masson was an inevitability, and the question should be not why Adler and Jung and Masson strayed from the fold but what, given their charac-ters, temperaments, and views of life, could have induced them to stray *into* the fold? (What it was about their char-acters, temperaments, and views of life that made them so attractive to precisely the people—Freud, Anna Freud, Eis-sler—who should have been most wary of them is another matter.) But if Masson was silent about—and possibly ig-norant of—the motive for his psychoanalytic volte-face, he was anything but reticent about the reversal of his fortunes that the Blumenthal articles brought about.

"When the *Times* articles appeared, in August of 1981, I was in Europe on one of my periodic trips for the Ar-chives," he told me. "After I returned to Berkeley, I imme-diately called Eissler, as I always did, to report on what I had done on my trip. I had found a lot of things in Anna Freud's house that I knew would interest him. I called his apartment, and his wife, Ruth Eissler, who is another emi-nent psychoanalyst, answered, and she was very cold. This had never happened before. Usually, there was a great com-motion—'Jeff, you're back! When will we see you?' This time, it was 'Kurt is busy now; he can't speak to you.' I said, 'It's Jeff, Jeff Masson!' 'Yes, I'm aware of that. Phone tomorrow.' Well, I thought, maybe she has a patient in the room with her and can't talk. I phoned the next day. 'No, he's still busy. Call tomorrow.' I thought, What is going on? This continues for four or five days—he's out, he's sick, his throat is sore, he has no voice left. Finally, at the end of five days, Eissler calls me, and he is in a rage. He starts shouting at me. 'Those articles—are you out of your mind? Do you know what this means?' And on and on and on. I said, 'Look, I'm sorry you didn't like the articles,' and Eissler said, 'You must write a letter immediately to the *Times* dissociating yourself from those views,' and I said, 'No, why should I? I don't think those articles are so bad. There are some things that got distorted, and I suppose I could write a letter about that. But, by and large, I don't think they're bad articles, and I believe the things I said. You've heard them from me many times before, and I don't see what the big deal is.' Well, Eissler continued to rant and rant, and finally I said, 'O.K., next time I'll be more careful,' and he said, *'There will be no next time!'* And I said, 'What do you mean?' He said, 'You were to be named my successor in November. Now I'm going to recommend to the Board that you be terminated.'

"I was in a state of shock. I had not expected that. I had given up my post at the University of Toronto a few months earlier—it's true that Eissler had urged me to hang on to it, but I saw no reason not to give it up. In November, I was to take over Eissler's position, and then, when Anna Freud died, I was to move to London and live in Anna Freud's house. Now, Eissler told me, I was finished. At the annual meeting of the Board, he would ask that my contract not be renewed. I said, 'I want to be present at that meeting. I want to hear what you will say.' Eissler said, 'No, no, it will be very humiliating and embarrassing. I don't want you to be humiliated and embarrassed.' I said, 'That's O.K. I can take care of myself.' Then Eissler said, 'What are you going to do now?' And I said, 'I'm going to sue you, probably.' He said, *'What?'* And I said, 'Well, of course. What did you think I was going to do—thank you for firing me? Why shouldn't I fight? You have no business getting rid of me. I haven't done anything wrong.' Then he said, 'I want my tapes back'—I had his tape-recorded interviews with hundreds of friends and colleagues and patients of Freud—and I said, 'That's too bad; I'm not going to give them back.' 'And I want all the letters back.' And I said, 'I'm not going to give them back, either.'

"After we hung up, I called Anna Freud. 'I have been fired from the Archives,' I told her, and she said, 'Well, I don't understand,' and I said, 'I have also been fired from the museum,' and she said, 'What museum?' I said, 'You know, I was going to live in your house.' She said, 'I never heard that.' I said, 'Come on, Eissler must have discussed it with you.' She said, 'No, he never discussed it with me. All he told me was that you were to be in charge of my father's library after my death. And, frankly, I would never have allowed you to live in my house, because my father would not have wanted someone like you living here. He would have wanted someone who was quiet and discreet.' She was quite honest about it, and I believed her. I knew she had complained endlessly to Muriel Gardiner about me. 'You don't know what it's like having Masson in my house,' she'd said. 'He's like my dogs.' She had these totally unmanageable chows—she'd inherited her father's chows, and these were their descendants—and she adored them. 'They race around the garden, they tear up everything, they get into everything. Masson is just like them.' "

During the five-day period when Masson was unable to get through to Eissler, he wrote Anna Freud a long letter of self-justification:

Sept. 2

Dear Miss Freud,

I have returned to a mountain of letters and innumerable messages. All because of the New York *Times* articles. Most of the response has been positive. But there have been some negative comments. Dr. Eissler, whom I have called several times but have not yet been able to reach (though I spoke to Ruth), is, I understand, very angry. Not at the first article, which he, like you, found harmless, but at the second. I must confess, I am puzzled. I realize that he (like most analysts) does not share my views about seduction. I continue to think that seduction, especially in its wholly negative aspect (i.e., rape and physical hurt), plays an important role in neurosegenesis. And I fully believe that trauma is at the very heart of illness. And, it is true, I do not believe that traumas, by and large, are invented. But I don't believe that this position is so very far removed from that held by your father. And I certainly do not draw any therapeutic conclusions from it. In any event, I do not practice analysis. I am merely a historian. It is true that I do not feel any particular obligation to the analytic community. My obligation, it seems to me, is entirely to historical truth. I have an enormous admiration for your father, and I think it shows in everything I write, and in the seriousness and zeal with which I pursue my research. But I do not feel the same admiration for the analytic movement and the analytic community. Perhaps for this reason, my research is almost exclusively devoted to the early history of Freud's progress. Surely that is my privilege. But I have never said anything, in print, to harm psychoanalysis as far as I can see. The fact that it does not interest me very much is of no concern to anybody except me. I certainly owe no loyalty to any other group, and I have, as everybody knows, nothing but contempt for the various movements that deviated from Freud's teachings.

I suppose I am writing to you now because we seem to have got on so well the last few times we met, and especially this last time. You have allowed me, in a show of great confidence, to go through your cupboard and, as you have seen, I found valuable and interesting material. I do not feel that I have or am likely to misuse this material in any way. Clearly, this has also been your feeling. But I know, too, that you do not expect me to hold to the standard view simply because it *is* the standard view when I find material that does not corroborate it. I am convinced that Freud did *not* abandon the seduction hypothesis in 1897, as has been commonly assumed.

Anna Freud replied on September 10 with a letter of characteristic calm, brevity, and intellectual incisiveness:

Dear Jeff Masson,

Your letter came today, and I answer quickly, since I may have to go to hospital in a few days, and that may mean an interruption. I am sorry, though, that my answer will be disappointing to you.

I have to tell you that I was also put off very much by the second article in the New York *Times,* only my reaction to it was different from Dr. Eissler's. I felt almost certain that the writer of the article had misunderstood you and that the interpretation concerning the seduction theory was his and not yours. I just could not imagine that it could be yours.

Of course, I have not read the lecture you gave in New Haven, but to me it seems out of the question that there is valid proof for the abandonment of the seduction theory for reasons of external rejection, nor can there be any valid sign that in spite of this abandonment it was kept up secretly. In fact, there is abundant proof to the contrary, not only in all the later case histories, but in the whole of the analytic theory altogether. *Keeping up the seduction theory would mean to abandon the Oedipus complex, and with it the whole importance of fantasy life, conscious or unconscious fantasy. In fact, I think there would have been no psychoanalysis afterwards* [italics added]. . . .

I know the Fliess letters so well, but I just cannot imagine what in them led you to this conclusion to which you have come.

I look forward to hearing more from you.

Yours sincerely,

Anna Freud

"The Board meeting—or should I say the witch trial?— was set for October fourteenth, at Eissler's apartment," Masson said, continuing the chronicle of his expulsion from the Archives. "In the weeks before the meeting, there were many telephone calls from Eissler. Some were very unpleasant, and others were warm and friendly. I couldn't figure out what was going on in his mind, except that he was in great conflict. He invited me to sleep at his apartment the night of the meeting, but I said no—I was going there to be fired, so I was not going to live in his house. He said, 'Well, let me pay for the expenses of the hotel.' I arrived at the meeting at eight, and Eissler took me aside and said, 'Do I have your word of honor that nothing we say here will ever go beyond these walls?' And I said, 'Of course you don't have my word.' 'In that case, I will have to ask you to leave,' he said. 'I have instructed the Board members not to speak unless you make that promise—that you give your word not to repeat anything that's said here to a lawyer, to the press, or to anyone.' He looked so unhappy, and it was such a deeply felt appeal, that I said, 'Well, let me think about it.' Then he was called away to the telephone, and when he came back he said, 'It's Muriel Gardiner. Before I speak to her, do I have your promise?' Muriel could not be at the meeting, because she was in the middle of the Atlantic on the *Queen Elizabeth*. She was clearly calling on my behalf—she had been very sympathetic to me—and I figured that this was Eissler's way of saying that once I agreed not to talk to the press, the Board members would say all is forgiven. So I said, 'All right, you have my promise.'

"The meeting began, and one of the first things said was 'Masson claims that psychoanalysis is sterile,' and everybody leaped up and was starting to jump on me when Eissler silenced them with a look and said, 'Fools, of course psychoanalysis is sterile,' and everybody sat down and said, 'Yes, yes, it's sterile, sir.' 'What I'm so enraged about,' Eissler went on, 'is that Masson should blame Freud for it,' and everybody leaped up again and said, 'Yes, yes, Freud.' Then Eissler lost his cool and started shouting for forty-five minutes. He was in a rage, he was trembling. Everybody was afraid he would collapse. He talked about my crazy theories, and how could I say what I said, and how could I do what I did, and how could anybody ever love me the way he had loved me, and had anyone ever done for me what he had done for me, and this is how I repay him. He went on and on, in a bizarre combination of personal confession, reproach, and ideological disagreement.

"Then I said, 'May I speak?' And Eissler said, 'Yes, yes,' and I defended myself for forty-five minutes, and then I said, 'I want to hear what the rest of you have to say. I want to know why I am being fired. What are the actual grounds?' And then everybody spoke in turn and voiced his objections to me, and they really had nothing to say, in effect, beyond trying to remember what Eissler had said. They all repeated something he had said. One analyst said, 'You showed poor judgment in giving that interview,' and I said, 'All right, suppose that's true—suppose I showed poor judgment. Is that any reason I shouldn't continue my work?' 'Yes, it's a very strong reason.' Another analyst said, 'Your picture appeared in the *Times*. No decent analyst would let his picture appear in the *Times*.'

"There was one very nice moment when Eissler was raging at me for having worn jeans when I went to see an old Swiss psychiatrist named Bleuler, from whom I was supposed to get some letters from Freud for the Archives. 'Look at your judgment, look at what you do!' Eissler said. 'You go see a distinguished member of an old family—the son of the great Bleuler who was the head of the Burghölzli— wearing bluejeans and a T-shirt. He is expecting to see a distinguished American professor, and you arrive looking like some hippie from California. How embarrassing! Of course you never got those letters.' And I said, 'I have news for you, Dr. Eissler. I did get them. Bleuler wrote to me last week that he will donate the letters.' And Eissler said bitterly, 'I am not surprised. You can charm anybody.' But, frankly, I was frightened. They kept hinting at 'the things we have against you.' It's frightening when thirteen serious men and women have decided that you're a real little shit, and they're going to tell you why. Eissler had said, 'It's going to be very embarrassing and humiliating for you,' and I was waiting for the axe to fall. What are they going to say about me? What have they found out? This is serious. They're going to fire me. But they never said anything— they never pointed to one thing I did that I could feel ashamed of.

"True, I acted stupidly from a political point of view. Last month, I saw Mark Paterson at the Frankfurt book fair, and he said to me, 'You dummy. You see what happened. Today, you and I would be driving back to London together. You would be moving into Anna Freud's house. Do you realize that all you had to do was keep your goddam mouth shut for another six months? Then you would have been in the Freud house, and you could have said anything you wanted to say, and no one could have touched you.' And no one could have. But I'm not sure I would have acted any differently even if I had known what the consequences would be. Because sooner or later the same thing would have happened. There would have been a rising tide of anger and resentment against me, with people demanding my resignation. True, it would have been very hard for them to get rid of me, and I wouldn't be under the financial stress I'm under now. But even if they had not tried to get me out I would have resigned and left the house within two or three years. Anyone who knows the things I know and believes the things I believe has no business being an analyst and describing himself as part of the profession.

"At one point in the meeting, I got really upset. Eissler said, 'I have always had to defend you against everyone who has ever met you. You are accused of being overzealous, overenthusiastic, tactless, indiscreet, *and* dishonest.' And I said, 'Just a minute. I resent that very much. I am not a dishonest person.' And Eissler said, 'No, I didn't say you were. I said that somebody accused you of it.' I said, 'I want to know who that is.' He said, 'All right, I'll tell you. It was Peter Swales.' Peter Swales is this completely off-the-wall young guy who writes these sensationalist papers about Freud. Then Eissler turned to the Board members and said, 'Of course, Peter Swales is paranoid.' I said, 'Fine—so now you're willing to tell the Board that the person who accuses me of dishonesty is paranoid.'

"The day after the meeting, I spoke to the *Times*, *Time*, and *Newsweek*. I said, 'Dr. Eissler forced me to promise him that I would not reveal anything that happened at the meeting. I'm sorry, gentlemen, that I have to go back on my word, but I will not be bound by such a promise.' Eissler had no business extracting that promise from me. He was always putting moral pressure on me. 'Do you want to poison Anna Freud's last days? Have you no heart? You're going to kill the poor old woman.' I said to him, 'What have I done? *You're* doing it. *You're* firing me. What am I supposed to do—be grateful to you?' 'You could be silent about it. You could swallow it. I know it is painful for you. But you could just live with it in silence.' 'Why should I do that?' 'Because it is the honorable thing to do.' Well, he had the wrong man."

Masson paused, and I said, "Tell me about Peter Swales." In the first Blumenthal article, Swales had been characterized as "a dogged Freud sleuth" who had unearthed an assertion by Fliess that Freud had plotted to murder Fliess by pushing him off a mountain during a walk, and who had come up with "controversial speculations . . . concerning, among other things, a possible love affair between Freud and his wife's unmarried sister, Minna Bernays." In a long article by David Gelman that appeared in the November 30, 1981, issue of *Newsweek,* entitled "Finding the Hidden

Freud," which covered some of the ground of the Blumenthal articles, pictures of Masson and Swales appeared side by side, under the caption "Masson, Swales: Impetuous Dissenters or Oedipal Ingrates?" Masson replied indifferently, "Swales used to work for me. He was very poor—his wife sold cookies in a bakery—so I gave him a few research projects to do. I'm a little sorry now I had anything to do with him. I don't like to see his name linked with mine. The difference between me and all the other Freud detractors is that they pick on some personal quirk—they're trivial. Who cares whether Freud slept with his sister-in-law? My point—that Freud sold out—is *not* trivial. To hear that Freud was a moral coward—that's more serious."

7

On August 26, 1981, the day after the second of the Blumenthal articles appeared in the *Times,* Eissler, at his summer place in Maine, wrote an angry and bitter letter to Masson, which, however, he did not mail. It reads, in part:

> I am very curious how the Archives Board will respond to your behavior. Your style is totally different from the Archives tradition, which is averse to publicity, was never used for personal aggrandizement of any participant, and was kept out of the reach of those who would have liked to use it for their particular brand of theory. You are always able to quiet me down when I try to show you how you provoke people and hurt them,

how indiscreet you are at times. I fear the members of
the Board will be soberer than I am. I heard so often in
the past that I am no good as a *Menschenkenner,* and I
foresee the necessity of admitting this weakness to the
Board in our October meeting. I know you will give me
again 100 reasons why and how you had to act, and how
things are distorted by others, and that the New York
Times article would have been far worse if you had not
interfered. I usually give in after 1 hr. telephone talk
and your promise that you will be careful and discreet.
I fear I am too old for that happy moment when you stop
blowing your horn. . . .

Let's wait and see whether the Board will be eager
to continue the contract with you.

At the previous year's meeting of the Board, Masson had
been appointed Projects Director of the Archives for one
year. According to the minutes (kept by the Secretary),

Dr. Eissler stated that in connection with the proposed publication of the Silberstein letters and the new
edition of the complete Fliess letters there should be a
person who could devote his time to these and perhaps
other forthcoming Archives projects. He suggested the
appointment for this purpose of Prof. J. M. Masson, a
41-year-old professor of Sanskrit, who is willing to give
up his professorship at the University of Toronto and
spend his time fully on Freud research. . . . He is a
charming person, knows analytical literature, and is
absolutely enthusiastic about the prospect of working on
projects related to Freud's biography. Prof. Masson's
salary ($30,000 per annum) would be covered by a con-
tribution from a friend of the Archives.

In the discussion that followed, Dr. [Sidney] Furst

expressed his reservations concerning Prof. Masson's discretion: he likes to talk and gossip, and may be indiscreet. . . .

Dr. [Peter] Neubauer interspersed at this point a cautionary note, saying that since it seems that Prof. Masson will play a significant role in the future of the Archives (especially if he moves to London to supervise the Freud Museum), it might be best to start him on a trial basis, and that the contract to employ him be made for one year, for a specific task, without further obligation. This course of action was agreed upon by the Board. . . .

Dr. Furst once again cautioned the Board members regarding Masson by saying that he writes well and is scholarly, but he is extreme in his positions.

On October 17, 1980, Eissler formally offered Masson the job of Projects Director. In his letter, he was a little untruthful. He wrote, "At its meeting on October 15th, the Board of Directors of the Sigmund Freud Archives instructed me to inquire whether you would be willing to serve for at least one year as Projects Director of the Archives." As the minutes of the meeting reveal, Eissler was instructed to offer Masson the job for *at most* one year. We are all perpetually smoothing and rearranging reality to conform to our wishes; we lie to others and to ourselves constantly, unthinkingly. When, occasionally—and not by dint of our own efforts but under the pressure of external events—we are forced to see things as they are, we are like naked people in a storm. There are a few among us—psychoanalysts have encountered them —who are blessed or cursed with a strange imperviousness to the unpleasantness of self-knowledge. Their lies to themselves are so convincing that they are never unmasked. These are the people who never feel in the wrong, who are always able to justify their conduct, and who in the end—human nature being what it is—cause their fallible fellow-men to turn away from them. Eissler is not such a person. His "lie" to Masson—the expression of his wish that his colleagues should like and trust his protégé more than they did—was too transparent to convince anyone, least of all Eissler himself. For Eissler admits to error so frequently, and with such almost childlike eagerness, that the admissions have become a sort of personal signature. His books and papers are filled with confessions of mistakes he believes he made and feels compelled to own up to. In *Medical Orthodoxy,* he berates himself for having supported (through the Archives) the research of a Professor Gicklhorn, who immediately turned around and, with his wife, wrote a book attacking Freud's character. "I deeply regret having contributed indirectly to this work," Eissler writes, "and wish to apologize, therefore, not only to members of the Board of the Sigmund Freud Archives, but also to any other colleagues who are interested in historical truth." In a 1963 paper entitled "Notes on the Psychoanalytic Concept of Cure," Eissler is critical of himself for having told an analytic patient that she must let him know before going on vacation whether she intended to come back for treatment in the fall—a not unreasonable demand, which most other analysts would feel justified in making. But in Eissler's considered opinion, "I'm not certain that my refusal to wait through the vacation for the young patient's decision was altogether wise." In a 1978 paper entitled "Creativity and Adolescence: The Effect of Trauma in Freud's Adolescence," he blames a chance remark he made to an adolescent patient for the boy's inability to pursue a career as a pianist. "At the end of the final interview, he asked me what he owed me. I told him, nothing, but that I should like to have 'two tickets, third row center' for his first concert at Carnegie Hall. Later, I heard that he had given up the instrument, not least because he had had the feeling that he would not be able to live up to the expectations I had expressed at our farewell." Eissler allows that the boy might have dropped out of music in any case, but he writes, "I doubt, however, that I can free myself completely from guilt for his abandoning a promising career. It is quite possible that my words burdened him with a great responsibility and he was crushed by an expectation he felt to be too great for him." Even Paul Roazen has not been exempt from Eissler's irrepressible urge to say he's sorry. During one of the polemical exchanges between Eissler and Roazen that have taken place in various journals since the publication of *Talent and Genius*—this one in the July 1977 issue of *Contemporary Psychoanalysis*—Eissler apologizes to Roazen for, among other things, doubting Roazen's good faith because he would not answer a letter in which Eissler proposed that their controversy be put before a panel of scholars appointed by the president of Harvard. Roazen had written in the January issue of *Contemporary Psychoanalysis,* "I ignored Eissler's letter [about the panel], since I regarded his request as an expression of embarrassing grandiosity. I cannot imagine the President of Harvard caring less about myself or the issues Eissler chooses to cook up." In his rejoinder, Eissler eagerly owns up to Roazen's charge of "embarrassing grandiosity." "Looking back, it is clear to me that this part of my proposal was not suitable, to say the least," he writes.

A final example of Eissler's remarkable freedom from self-justification comes from one of the case histories in his 1955 book *The Psychiatrist and the Dying Patient*. He treated a wealthy older woman during the years before her death, and was so helpful to her that, in gratitude, she changed her will and left him a huge amount of money. Eissler was totally unprepared for and "painfully surprised" by this development. "It was evident that the acceptance of any benefit derived from a patient's will would be unethical, and I informed the attorney that my legacy had to be distributed among the other legatees or given to charitable institutions, whatever might be the proper procedure," he writes. However, a Mr. X, the husband of a relative of the deceased whose legacy had been diminished because of the change in the will, formally objected to the probation of the will. He happened to be an analyst, and his argument was that Eissler had exercised "undue influence" on the patient through "the unconscious utilization of a transference." Eissler laconically mentions that "the matter was settled" but then, over many pages, ponders Mr. X's charge from the legal, moral, and psychoanalytic points of view, and finally concludes that it had merit. "The austerity which the therapist must impose on the patient must be equally valid for himself, and he cannot enjoy some of the benefits which other professions are permitted to enjoy," he writes. "Therefore, I made a mistake when I initially thought my bequest could be used for charitable purposes. Even if this could be done in strict anonymity, without any benefit to the therapist's prestige, it still would have been against a self-evident and therefore unwritten basic principle." The case history ends with a wonderful twist. Eissler gradually comes to believe that the patient's apparently loving gesture was in fact an expression of her hatred of him—an expression of the negative transference that had never been allowed to emerge during the treatment. "She was a woman of the world, quite aware of the ill repute in which some people hold psychiatry and psychoanalysis, precisely because of the allegation that monetary interests play a prominent role in these specialties. Not only must she have known that I would never accept her legacy, but she must also have been aware of the danger and suspicion to which she exposed me. With particular finesse, under the guise of a special favor, she made me the victim of an ambivalence which must have dated far back in our relationship."

Eissler has subjected his relationship with Jeffrey Masson to the same self-unsparing scrutiny. When, a few weeks after returning from Berkeley, I spoke with him in his office, he said, "I search myself for my ambivalence toward Freud. To have put someone like Masson in a position where he might become Secretary of the Archives! To have made such a blunder at the end of the game! I wouldn't listen to anybody. Even my own secretary warned me about him." Eissler sat behind his huge, unbelievably disorderly desk—on which papers, books, journals, newspapers, letters were strewn like an adolescent's clothing—and I sat facing him. His back was to a window through which the dark, bare trees of Central Park swayed and the lights of the East Side glowed faintly.

"But isn't there another explanation?" I said. "That you were fond of him and wouldn't hear ill spoken of him?"

"The homosexual explanation," Eissler said. "Yes, he had great homosexual appeal, strong appeal. Not that I ever had any homosexual fantasies about him. But I find the homosexual explanation even worse. I prefer the other explanation."

"He still can't accept being fired," I said. "His narcissism was wounded when you withdrew your approval."

"Well, my narcissism was wounded when I was proved to be a fool! You know how my colleagues feel about me after this."

"You had no doubts about him before the *Times* articles?" I asked.

"I am guilty," Eissler said. "I was taken in. I thought he was a godsend. I had long wanted to retire from the Archives, and here was just the right man. He was young and idealistic, he had trained as an analyst for ten years, he was dedicated to psychoanalysis, he knew German, he was full-time. What a plum, I thought. So he had some faults. I saw them. I wasn't that big a fool. But everybody has faults. I made excuses for him. He was young. There was an incident when he offered to give material to another young scholar, Peter Swales, which he had no business offering him. But I gave him another chance. I have been accused of being too rigid; I thought, I will not behave rigidly in this. He talked too much. I would always know his itinerary when he travelled, because I would get telephone calls wherever he went from people complaining about him. I continued to make excuses. But finally, when those newspaper articles came out, it gradually dawned on me that this was an impossible situation. Don't you agree with me? Am I really crazy when I have the impression that someone who says that the sterility of psychoanalysis was caused by Freud isn't the right person to be Secretary of the Freud Archives?" Eissler paused, then added, "He was always pleasant and nice to me. He would give me presents. He was mean to others. Then, finally, he was mean to me. He wouldn't give me back the tapes I had made over thirty years, which I had given him to transcribe. I had to sue to get them back."

8

CREATIVE work in any established system of thought takes place at the boundaries of the system, where its powers of explanation are least developed and its vulnerability to outside attack is most marked. Since the death of Freud, the most original work done in psychoanalysis has been in and around the area of "object relations" theory, which traces the origin of the severer neuroses and of the psychoses to disturbances of the relationship between mother and child in the earliest period of life, known as the pre-Oedipal period. Michael Balint, D. W. Winnicott, M. Masud R. Khan, W. R. D. Fairbairn, Margaret Mahler, Heinz Kohut, and Selma Fraiberg are among the analysts who have toiled in this mired field and who, from their various perspectives, have struggled to imaginatively reconstruct the world of the infant who has not received the comfort, stimulation, and security—the "good-enough mothering"—on which good-enough mental functioning is thought to depend. That these innovators are working at the edge of psychoanalytic theory is evident from two common aspects of their thought: its downgrading of the Oedipus complex as the central formative experience of childhood, and its emphasis on actuality— on the glaring facts of maternal deprivation and abuse. It is here—at this edge—that the movement within psychoanalysis that seeks to expand the limits of Freud's theory merges with the external movement that seeks to undermine it, to the consternation of both sides. When Freud dropped the seduction theory and introduced the theories of infantile sexuality and the Oedipus complex, he transformed psychoanalysis from a form of social psychiatry into a depth psychology. The seduction theory had to do with the impact of manifest environmental evils on people's mental balance; the theories of infantile sexuality and the Oedipus complex were elements in a radical and quite fantastical conception of human nature which says we are ruled (and sometimes unhinged) by events that we only imagined as small children—and that, moreover, we were unconscious, and remain unconscious, of having imagined. Although Freud came to believe that many or most of the seductions reported by his patients were "wishful fantasies," he never doubted that seductions and rapes and beating of children sometimes do take place. It is simply that as he grew more and more fascinated and preoccupied by his universal psychology he grew less and less interested in the special plight of the people to whom unspeakable things happen. These psychoanalytic foundlings have once again become objects of interest—to the innovative analysts who are seeking to expand psychoanalytic theory and technique to embrace patients much sicker than those whom Freud was content to treat. Although these analysts are hardly interested in reviving the seduction theory, and are scarcely of the opinion that psychoanalysis died a premature death when Freud abandoned that theory, they and Masson—embarrassingly and confusingly—find themselves on the same side of the fence in the debate concerning "reality" which has polarized psychoanalysis since its earliest days.

It is all very slippery. Even orthodox analysts who have no intention of venturing anywhere near the abyss of revisionism can lose their bearings and find themselves at its brink. A case in point is that of the analyst William Niederland and his research on the Schreber case. In 1903, a book was published in Germany called *Memoirs of My Nervous*

Illness, by Daniel Paul Schreber, which attracted a good deal of attention in psychiatric circles because of its richly specific description of the author's bizarre paranoid delusional system and of the exquisite mental sufferings he experienced while under its sway. Schreber had been a lawyer and a judge before his breakdown and incarceration in an insane asylum, and he wrote his book as part of a legal struggle to regain his freedom. It was published—over the protest of his relatives, who severely censored the manuscript—after his release. Sigmund Freud was among those fascinated by the Schreber memoirs, and in 1911 he published a paper analyzing Schreber on the basis of his book and using his case to illustrate the thesis that at the core of male paranoia lies a homosexual conflict. (Schreber's dominating delusion was that he had to change into a woman in order to fulfill his mission as redeemer of the world.) Freud never met Schreber and knew almost nothing about him or his family except what he could glean from the *Memoirs,* and this was very little, because of the censorship exercised by the relatives. In the fifties, Niederland began to delve into the background of Schreber. It was known that Schreber's father had been a distinguished physician and educator who wrote numerous books on child-rearing, and Niederland had the idea of reading some of these books. What he found was horrifying. Schreber *père* was revealed as a tyrant and a sadist, and the childhood of Schreber *fils* (and his sisters and brother) as a nightmare of physical and mental oppression, imposed in the name of the father's Teutonic educational ideals. The most horrifying of Niederland's findings, and those most directly relevant to Paul Schreber's craziness, concerned the father's invention of orthopedic devices involving straps, belts, and iron bars for the straightening of children's posture. In the light of Niederland's discoveries, some of Paul Schreber's most mystifying delusional experiences, which he called "miracles," began to make sense. For example, his "compression-of-the-chest miracle"—which, he writes in the *Memoirs,* "I endured at least several dozen times; it consisted in the whole chest wall being compressed, so that the state of oppression caused by the lack of breath was transmitted to my whole body"—clearly derived from a device called "the straightener," which Niederland describes as consisting of "a system of iron bars fastened to the chest of the child as well as to the table near which the child was sitting; the horizontal iron bar pressed against the chest and prevented any movement forward or sideward, giving only some freedom to move backward to an even more rigidly upright position." Other "miracles" derived from other cruel devices, as well as from various features of the father's dire program to eradicate all ease and comfort from his children's lives, lest they grow soft.

Niederland, an orthodox New York analyst, presented his findings as a reverent amplification of Freud's paper rather than as a challenge to it. Nowhere does he suggest that Freud's analysis of Schreber would have been in any way different if Freud had known what Niederland now knew, and this has remained the orthodox Freudian position on the Schreber case. However, in 1973 Morton Schatzman, a young American psychiatrist living in England, published a book called *Soul Murder: Persecution in the Family,* which drew heavily on Niederland's research but did a good deal more than murmur, "My, how interesting!," as Niederland had done. "Christ, how appalling!" is the tone of Schatzman's book, which proposes a clear cause-and-effect relationship between the oppression of the child and the madness

of the man. In the light of the new information, Schatzman
—then a follower of the anti-psychiatry movement of R. D.
Laing, which stressed the impact of reality on mental illness,
with particular emphasis on the family—regarded Freud's
thesis about Schreber's repressed homosexual feelings toward his father as a preposterous irrelevancy. *Soul Murder*
put the Freudian establishment in a serious bind: here was
an odious (to the Freudians) anti-psychoanalytic book that
could not be dismissed, since it was based on the research
of a Freudian analyst. In their efforts to discredit Schatzman
without discrediting Niederland, the Freudians gave the
impression of being strapped into one of Schreber *père*'s
contrivances. They wiggled and squirmed and couldn't free
themselves. They were finally reduced to such absurdities
as calling Schatzman's honesty into question for using Niederland's research (as if it were honorable to use secondary
sources only if you agree with their author), and even to
employing some sharp practices of scholarship. A fast one
was pulled by Niederland himself. Responding to Schatzman's accusation that "although Freud knew of Schreber's
father, he did not use his writings as data, even though the
father's books had been widely read and are still available,"
Niederland charged Schatzman with ignoring "the policy
of restraint" that Freud announced he was following in his
paper in order to spare the feelings of Schreber, his family,
and his psychiatrist, Paul Emil Flechsig. In Freud's text,
however, "the policy of restraint" has nothing to do with
the feelings of Schreber, his relatives, or his psychiatrist, or
with any issue of discretion whatever; it simply (and plainly)
refers to the intellectual strategy that Freud proposes to
adopt in order to make sure that his reasoning can be followed. (Niederland's inexplicable misreading of Freud was

pointed out by the Dutch writer Han Israëls in his brilliant book *Schreber, Father and Son,* as yet unpublished here, which demonstrates that practically everyone who has ever written about Schreber and his father has been off the mark by distances ranging from an inch to a mile.)

It was in this context that Jeffrey Masson wrote his 1974 paper "Schreber and Freud: A Review of 'Soul Murder,'" which he read at the spring meeting of the American Psychoanalytic Association, in Denver. It now seems almost inevitable that Masson should have gravitated toward the Schreber case. The trouble the Freudians had had with Schatzman was like a dress rehearsal for the trouble they were going to have with Masson. In both cases, men with a profound antipathy to psychoanalysis sought corroboration in historical material for their view that we are ruled by external reality rather than by our inner demons; and in both cases the psychoanalytic establishment proved unequal to the task of making the Freudian position cogent. Since Masson in 1974 was still aspiring to be an analyst (he was in his fourth year of training at Toronto), his Schreber paper was a kind of tour de force of talking out of both sides of his mouth: While apparently holding to the official view of Schatzman as a disreputable "popularizer," he in fact fully agreed with Schatzman's major point that in the cruelty of the father lies *the* explanation for the illness of the son.

One afternoon in the winter of 1983, I spoke with Leonard Shengold, the analyst who nine years earlier, at the Denver meeting, had characterized Masson as one of Canada's national treasures. Shengold occupies a special corner in the analytic avant-garde. On the one hand, he shares the avant-garde's concern for "people who have been unloved, ill-used, and deprived" (as he writes in a paper entitled

"Child Abuse and Deprivation: Soul Murder"), but, on the other, he does not share its (variously expressed) need to meddle with orthodox theory and practice. Almost alone among analysts who have dedicated themselves to the repair of seriously damaged souls, Shengold has remained comfortable with regular Freudian psychoanalysis. He disagrees with the purists' contention that it doesn't matter what really happened. (In "Child Abuse and Deprivation," he writes, "The patient must know what he has suffered, at whose hands, and how it has affected him. The means he uses to not know, to deny, must be made fully conscious.") But he would agree with the New Haven analyst who illustrated the awesome variety of human experience with the extreme example of the boy who felt that Auschwitz had made a man of him. "I have seen that even the predominantly soul-destroying experiences of incest seem in some cases to be modified by soul-saving aspects—the child making use of some phases of the sexual contact to fulfill the need for attention and tenderness," Shengold writes in "Child Abuse." "It is in no way to condone or minimize the often heartbreaking damage done to observe that some victims of soul murder seem to have been strengthened by the terrible experiences they have endured. Talents and, occasionally, creative power can arise from a background of soul murder."

To me, Shengold said, "I found it very exciting to hear some of the things I had felt about the Schreber case, and particularly about Schreber's father, emphasized by Jeff. At the meeting, Niederland delivered some prepared comments on Jeff's paper, and he played down the disturbance in Schreber's father. He minimized it, saying he wouldn't necessarily call the man psychotic or an evil influence, which seemed to me to show a mind-boggling lack of imagination. So I stood up to defend Jeff. I didn't know him at all. I thought, Who is this guy? I've never heard of him before and he's challenging Niederland, one of the father figures in my institute and a famous name in psychoanalysis. I thought, Good for him! But, as I got to know him better, more of what I saw gave me pause." Shengold is a heavyset, soft-spoken man in his late fifties, a thoughtful, serious person, more widely read than the average analyst, and also slightly more obsessive about the fine points of analytic etiquette: during my talks wth him in his office he was always looking at his watch to make sure a patient wasn't being kept waiting. "What bothered me about Jeff was that he seemed to be courting the favor of anyone who could do anything for him—and in a way that was so open that it had a kind of breathtaking honesty. He made no bones about it. He seemed to feel that he was entitled to the regard of these people. And he was so likable that one accepted it as a kind of joke. But it took me aback, because it not only made me distrust him as an observer but revealed a vein of immaturity, which could be perfectly compatible with his being a brilliant and reliable person but not with his being an analyst. And the way he would argue, the certainties he had! To be an analyst and to be certain—they don't go together. You have to have doubts. You have to be capable of certainty, too, but it has to be hedged with doubt. What you learn as an analyst is how much you don't know. I don't think Jeff would have got through our institute." Shengold glanced at his watch, and went on, "Let me say this about Jeff's trauma theory. It fits in so well with most patients' resistances —resistances not just to analysis but to the responsibility for one's own inner life: 'Look what they did to me!' Yet we are all traumatized to some extent, and the need to deny what we believe actually happened (and what may indeed have happened) is also universal. It's not a simple business. To mediate between what Ernst Kris called personal myth—a defensive re-creation of the past—and the denial or non-registration of the past is always difficult, and sometimes impossible. The holocausts—public and private—did and do occur. They are hard to register. But they do not explain everything. Neurosis has turned out to be the human condition, and not just the result of 'seduction by the father.'" Shengold looked at his watch for the third time, and said, "I'm going to have to stop in four minutes. What happened to Jeff at the Archives was unfortunate. He very much needs the acceptance and corroboration of people he respects. He wants desperately to have ties to people like Eissler. These connections give him narcissistic nourishment, and when he doesn't get it, it's a terrible strain for him. He provoked what happened, of course, but it's terribly unfortunate that he elicited all this reaction from Anna Freud and Eissler and the whole psychoanalytic establishment. It pushed him in an unhealthy direction. There's a kind of crazy sincerity there, but he can turn against anyone, because he can feel betrayed by anyone."

I said, "He feels that Eissler betrayed him by firing him."

"Eissler betrayed him by suddenly looking at him and seeing what he was. That's a fatal sin." Shengold paused, then said, "Eissler may have been attracted to Jeff in somewhat the way Freud was attracted to Fliess. Fliess was a very charming and vivacious man, and Freud had a need and a terrible weakness for that kind of glamorous person. When Jung came along, he became that person again for Freud. Both Fliess and Jung were charlatans in some ways, but very bright, very beguiling ones. There must have been something of that sort going on between Eissler and Jeff. But there was something else. Eissler is such an isolated and lonely person.

Everybody respects him, but nobody will approach him, because they're a little afraid of him. He has a standoffish manner. But Jeff approached him in a very friendly and interested way, and Eissler responded immediately. Eissler doesn't think he's lovable. I have the feeling that he doesn't have close friends. He seems desperate for a kind of friendliness that he cannot achieve naturally and spontaneously. And he found it in Jeff."

PART II

I

No single explanation can really explain human behavior; it can at most illuminate human behavior and allow us to see something we had not seen. . . . An accident may be considered a paradigm. Why did it happen? The road was icy at that point. And the driver of the small car was in a great hurry because he was late for a crucial appointment, because the person who had promised to pick him up had not come. And his reflexes were slower than usual because he had had hardly any sleep that night because his mother had died the day before. And just before the accident his attention was distracted for one crucial second by a very pretty girl on the side of the road, who reminded him of a girl he had once known. Yet he might have regained control of his car if only a truck had not come toward him just as he skidded into the left lane. The truck driver might have managed not to hit him, but . . . If we add that the truck driver had just gone through a red light and was, moreover, going much faster than the legal speed limit, the policeman who witnessed the accident, as well as the court later on, might discount as irrelevant everything said before the three dots and be quite content to explain the accident simply in terms of the truck driver's two violations. He caused the accident. But that does not rule out the possibility that the other driver had a strong death wish because his mother had died, or that he punished himself for looking at an attractive girl the way he did so soon after his mother's death, or that the person who had let him down was partly to blame. —Discovering the Mind, Vol. III: Freud v. Adler and Jung, by Walter Kaufmann.

The question of why Masson queered his chances with the Archives—why he all but forced Eissler to see what Eissler had been carefully trying to not see during the decade of their acquaintance, and why he acted as he did when he could have quietly bided his time until he actually had power in hand—has been asked by many observers of the events of the summer and fall of 1981, and is almost invariably answered in terms of some need of Masson's for self-destruction. The form of the question practically dictates the answer; implicit in it is the assumption that Masson acted as a free agent—that he had choices, that he was responding to inner rather than to external pressures. But there is another way of looking at Masson's fall from favor—the way of the melodramatist, who views human conduct as a mechanical response to the inexorable pressure of events set in motion by the malign motives of others. This is the view of Peter Swales, who holds himself responsible for setting in motion a series of actions that culminated in the fatal interview in the *Times* —the event that undid Masson with Eissler. Four months earlier, in April, Swales had written Masson a letter in which —for *forty-five single-spaced typewritten pages*—he enumerated the wrongs he felt he had suffered at Masson's hands, and spewed forth the hatred, anger, and contempt he felt for him. The letter, a kind of masterpiece of invective, was written not only, and not even mainly, to its addressee but to a circle of friends, acquaintances, and enemies to whom Swales regularly sends Xerox copies of his epistolary productions, and also to any potential chronicler of the Swales-Masson quarrel who might someday materialize. "I imagined that if I compressed all these objections to Masson into one form, if I made a big snowball of it, I could get that snowball in motion," Swales told this chronicler, who had materialized on cue. He continued, "I felt that if I invested enough, so to speak, conscious energy in it, my letter would acquire the status of a historical document. I thought, If I write this forty-five-page account of what happened between Masson and me, it will be like a piece of rock, and I can hurl it at him, and who knows what it will put in motion? And, sure enough, a chain of events was set off that climaxed in the Blumenthal articles."

Swales is a small, delicately constructed man of thirty-five who looks ten years younger; he has a pert, fresh face and straight light-brown hair that keeps falling in his eyes and that he keeps pushing back in a tense, unconscious gesture. One would not extrapolate this agreeable youth from the dire antagonist in the letter to Masson. Nor would one easily believe that this watchful boy, this pensive Peter Pan, was one of the world's leading authorities—perhaps *the* leading authority—on the early life of Freud and on the early history of psychoanalysis. How Swales—who is not an analyst or a Ph.D., or even a high-school graduate—came to achieve this status in the world of Freud scholarship is a story that that world has yet to digest. Swales tells it thus in a *curriculum vitae* he wrote in 1980:

I was born in 1948 in Haverfordwest, on the south-west tip of Wales. My parents are the proprietors of a specialist music-and-record store in that town. From the age of eleven I attended grammar-school there and, on account of my consistently high performance, a splendid academic career was forecast for me. However, the spiritual bankruptcy of the educational system to which I was exposed; the cultural and intellectual impoverishment of my native milieu; and various other factors, including an unfavorable constellation of family dynamics —all these conspired in 1965 to bring about an abrupt and premature end to my school career. I left my home town and went to live in London.

The next seven years I spent working in the gramophone-record industry—first as a trainee in the sales division of a large record company; then as factotum for a small but successful record company; then as personal assistant to the famous group of musicians the Rolling Stones. . . . But during these years, more or less as a hobby, I also gave attention to those areas of interest toward which I am naturally and spontaneously inclined —namely, psychology, philosophy, and the history of ideas.

In 1971–72, with the demise of my activities in the music industry, I found myself in a position to be able to devote some time to private study. I took full advantage of the opportunity by procuring an entry ticket to the British Museum Reading Room and immersing myself for the best part of a year in various historical and psychological literature.

In mid-1972, I decided to move to New York, where an American whom I had known for some years offered me a position as director of a new, independent book-publishing venture, which he was in the throes of launching, called the Stonehill Publishing Company. In 1973, I negotiated North American publication of a series of early scientific papers by Sigmund Freud that were concerned with the drug cocaine. Dr. Robert Byck, professor of psychopharmacology at the Yale University School of Medicine, was appointed editor of the volume, and over a period of six months I assisted him in compiling and editing an anthology consisting of these and many other related writings. It was the knowledge gained through my private studies during these years, 1971–73, that gave me the intellectual preparation necessary for approaching the work of Freud. And, rather to my surprise, in this particular sphere of history and ideas I found myself very much at home. . . .

I had telephoned Swales after my return from Berkeley, and he had taken to coming to my house in the afternoon, first in order to acquaint me with the particulars of his quarrel with Masson, and then, as time went on, to speak about his work and his past and his philosophy of life. He was always free in the afternoon. He goes to bed late, writing until two or three in the morning, and gets up at eleven or twelve. He lives in a tenement on Mott Street with his German-born wife, Julia, a painter, who works as the manager of a pastry shop. When Swales awakes, he throws on some clothes and goes padding lightly down four flights of stairs to the mailbox, which is almost always full. Letters from all over the world arrive daily—from scholars, professors, psychoanalysts, psychiatrists, sociologists, writers, graduate students, librarians, archivists, journalists. When he came to my house, he would often bring a thick loose-leaf notebook filled with letters that he had culled from his files for the occasion, and he would read out passages from them as he spoke, like a lecturer showing slides. He told me that, unlike most people, who enter the psychoanalytical world through the experience of analysis or the reading of Freud, he had entered it "by the back door, so to speak, of the drug culture." One day shortly after he took up his duties at the Stonehill Publishing Company, he was browsing in a secondhand bookstore and came across a little out-of-print volume called *The Cocaine Papers,* which he thought might be of interest to the president of Stonehill, the late Jeffrey Steinberg, who was a heroin addict and cocaine user. The book was a collection of Freud's early writings on cocaine; during the eighteen-eighties, Freud had hoped to make his fame and fortune by developing medical uses for the drug, and he was then also an enthusiastic recreational user of it. Swales's idle find led to the republication by Stonehill of Freud's cocaine papers, under Robert Byck's editorship. While the book was being prepared for the press, Swales fell out with Steinberg, quit Stonehill, and decided to write a book of his own on Freud's involvement with cocaine. "I was totally fascinated with the phenomenon of drug-taking," Swales said. "It horrified me. I was never into drugs in a big way myself, but there had been many times in my life when I was in the company of guys who were tripped out on LSD or cocaine, and I was totally fascinated. My fascination was consummated with Freud." Swales said that he "reluctantly" began to read Freud's writings as preparation for his book on Freud and cocaine—a project that he abandoned as his interest gradually shifted from the phenomenon of drug-taking to the person of Freud. "I began to see that Freud was not the virtuous and straightforward man he has been pictured as being," he said to me. Swales received his first whiff of what he called Freud's "deviousness" when he read the paper "Screen Memories" (1899), which contains a piece of hidden autobiography: the "patient" in the paper who tells the analyst of a childhood memory that the analyst interprets as a mask for a later sexual fantasy is Freud himself. ("It was not difficult to guess that the incident described in it was in fact an autobiographical one, and this became a certainty after the appearance of the Fliess correspondence," James Strachey, the editor of the Standard Edition of Freud's works, writes in his introduction to the paper.) "That to me was just mind-blowing," Swales said. "I mean, the standard portrait of Freud is always that of a man of flawless integrity, and here was a blatant example of his abuse of the reader's good faith." Swales began to look for other examples of covert autobiography in Freud's writings. In 1976, he returned to his parents' house in Wales, and he spent the next four years constructing what he calls "my Freud universe," buttressing his inferences about "the man behind the mask" with facts drawn first from published biographical sources (such as the Jones biography and the Freud-Fliess letters) and then from archives, police blotters, cure lists from health spas, timetables, newspapers, and interviews with the descendants of onetime patients and colleagues of Freud.

Swales's *curriculum vitae* continues:

Back in Haverfordwest, I began actively pursuing historical researches into the life of Freud and the early history of psychoanalysis. By 1977, I had begun corresponding with the descendants of many persons of importance in the Freud world and also with persons in various parts of Europe who were in a position—physically and professionally speaking—to follow up specific

research projects instigated by myself. Between 1977 and
1979, I undertook four extensive journeys across Central
Europe, twice beyond the Iron Curtain, in order to
personally pursue certain avenues of investigation. A
fuller explanation of my work, and a description of its
present status, is to be found in the attached research
program. . . .

The *curriculum vitae* and the "attached research program" were part of an application (successful in May 1980)
for a grant of seven thousand dollars from Muriel Gardiner's
New-Land Foundation. The architect of the arrangement
was Kurt Eissler. The story of how Eissler came to be
Swales's sponsor is one that Swales tells with great satisfaction (and that Eissler shudders to recall). What brought
the two together was a mysterious "mistake" made by the
Library of Congress. In 1978, Eissler bought for the Archives
(for the sum of a hundred thousand dollars, donated by
Muriel Gardiner), from a Mr. Stanescu, who had smuggled
them out of Rumania, the letters of Freud to his boyhood
friend Eduard Silberstein. Eissler deposited the letters in the
Library of Congress, where, he assumed, they would lie un-
disturbed with the rest of the entombed treasure. But, for a
reason never explained, the Library listed the bulk of the
Silberstein letters in the unrestricted section of its catalogue
of the Archives' holdings. (Some items in the Archives have
long been available to the general public.) In the summer
of 1979, Swales—then deep in his research on Freud's early
life and chafing under the restrictions of the Archives—received a copy of the Library of Congress catalogue, and
could hardly believe his eyes when they fell on the Silberstein
listing. "But what does a guy in my position do?" he said to

me. "He doesn't ask questions. He writes off to the Library and asks for Xerox copies. And, sure enough, in a couple of months this great big wad of stuff arrives in the mail—what amounted to two-thirds of the Silberstein letters—together with a letter saying, 'Please address yourself to Dr. K. R. Eissler, of the Sigmund Freud Archives, for permission to see the other one-third, which is restricted.' I did not immediately write to Eissler for permission—I went to Germany to work with two Freud scholars in Tübingen—and by the time I did write him, in the winter of 1980, he already knew I had the letters; a clergyman from Strasbourg, whom I had met in Tübingen and to whom I had shown a few of them, had told him. Eissler was very puzzled and confused. He couldn't understand how I had got the Silberstein letters. He wrote and said, 'I have no idea how you got those letters. I was never asked about it, and would never have given permission.' I had returned to New York by then, and wrote back saying, 'Look, this is ridiculous. You're telling me that I'm not supposed to have those letters, and I do have them—the Library of Congress sent them to me. Why don't we meet and sort this out?' Eissler agreed, and I went up to Central Park West to see him. Of course, I was aware of him through the literature, and I was fascinated to meet him. I wanted to find out who the man really was. On the one hand, I had certain prejudices, you might say. I mean, my God, the guy has to be nuts—the way he's written six articles and a whole book against Roazen, for instance. On the other hand, I did very much respect him. He's a great thinker, potentially, even though his starting premises are wrong. He has done Freud scholarship a good service in, say, replying to the Gicklhorns.

"I went up to his place and explained the situation about

the Silberstein letters. We had this brisk, sort of bitchy exchange. 'Well, Dr. Eissler!' 'Well, Mr. Swales!' And after about five minutes it suddenly fell flat. There was literally this long silence. And then, somewhat grudgingly, Eissler said, 'Well, anyway, Mr. Swales, why are you so interested in this stuff?' And I said, 'I'm totally fascinated with the life and work of Freud, and I've done a lot of research.' 'Like what?' Eissler said. 'What have you found?' His attitude was challenging. 'Well, I've worked with Professor Sajner in Moravia, and Professor Fichtner and Dr. Hirschmüller in Tübingen,' and one thing and another, you know. And then it started to get specific. Like 'What did you find in Moravia?' 'I got Dr. Sajner to dig up all the cure lists at Roznau.' [These lists showed that Freud's mother went every year to the Roznau spa, possibly to meet a lover, Swales speculates.] Eissler said, 'You did? That's incredible!' Then Freud's patients in *Studies on Hysteria* came up. 'Whom have you researched?' Eissler asked. 'Well, for instance, Katharina,' I said. 'I have identified her.' 'No! I don't believe it! I sent a man to that mountain years ago, and he failed where you have succeeded. And Freud's patient Cäcilie M., who was she?' I told him, and he was flabbergasted. Everything I said was news to him. I couldn't believe what was happening, because I wasn't gunning for it, but the next thing I knew, he was saying, 'Mr. Swales, how much money would you need to complete your research?' I said, 'I don't know, I'd have to think about it,' and he said, 'Well, I can get you four thousand dollars. Write me a prospectus, and I'll get you the money.' I went out of that building and I phoned my wife and I said, 'Julia, you won't believe this. It's crazy.'

"There was an irony to my getting involved with Eissler.

I thought, If and when the day comes that I publish my thesis on Freud's love affair with Minna Bernays, Eissler is going to be in a strange position. How will he be able to repudiate my scholarship when he has invested in it? I was ready to exploit that irony. I was playing my cards very carefully. I wouldn't go so far as to call it conniving, but I certainly entertained the idea that in winning Eissler's confidence I might get to learn what he had in the Archives, what he was holding back.

"By now, I was working on a biography of Wilhelm Fliess, along with my Freud work. This came about in the following way: In 1978, I happened to find out the address of Fliess's daughter, who was living in Israel in an old folks' home under her married name. Her name is Pauline Jacobsohn, and nobody knew she was still alive. So I went to Israel, and she led me to an archive in the Hebrew University, in Jerusalem, where she had deposited her father's literary estate. When I saw this material, this *Nachlass*—it was in boxes piled that high—I had to reconcile myself to the fact that I was going to write a biography of Fliess. Finding this *Nachlass* put me in a, so to speak, very powerful position—not that I was looking for power. Now, here is where Masson comes into the story." Swales paused to thumb through his thick loose-leaf notebook, which lay between us on the table at which we sat drinking tea, and then read from a letter he had written to Pauline Jacobsohn on January 24, 1980:

Dear Mrs. Jacobsohn:
    A short while back, I learned from the scholar Frank Sulloway that Anna Freud has commissioned an American psychoanalyst, Dr. Jeff Masson, of Berkeley, Cali-

fornia, to edit a volume of the complete letters of Freud to your father, to be published in seven to ten years' time. I plan within the next few weeks to write to Masson asking him if he would kindly clarify some important points with respect to your father's life and work and his association with Freud in the light of those Freud letters still to be published. Like Anna Freud, Masson refused to give any information to Sulloway, so I can be pretty sure he will not oblige me either. However, I strongly suspect he would fast change his tune and coöperate if I were to mention in a second letter that I happen to know of the whereabouts of a few unknown and unpublished letters from the Freud-Fliess correspondence (namely, those letters donated by you to the Hebrew University).

Of course, this strategy can be effective only so long as Masson and the other members of the Freud establishment (e.g., Dr. Eissler) remain unaware of the existence of all that material. I would be most grateful if, at least for the next few months, you would kindly refrain from mentioning the material in Jerusalem. If my contact with you was known, then Masson would straightaway guess where to look for those few letters of Freud to Fliess (as mentioned above), and before long he would surely turn up at your door asking to be told more. Oh, how complicated things get! But all this arises out of the Freud establishment's selective employment of historical material towards perpetuating and enhancing the Freud myth at the expense of persons such as Fliess. They have never done Fliess's memory any favors. The biographical work now in preparation will provide a valuable corrective. But it is important that this time, in terms of new material, "we," and not the Freud establishment, have, as it were, the upper hand.

Pauline Jacobsohn wrote back a few weeks later, saying bluntly:

> What you write about Mr. Masson is not very nice. It depends on how and for what he asks, if at all he will write to me. I cannot lie to him, and don't forget my age. It does not allow such manipulations.

In reply, Swales apologized for "having made this suggestion and upset you," and then added,

> I now have a little surprise to tell you: Only two days after I wrote to Masson requesting information on your father from the as yet unpublished letters of Freud (in other words, well before he received my letter to him), I received a letter from Germany in which Masson asked if *I* can be of assistance to *him!* He learned of my address through a doctor in Vienna who knew of various investigations I have made into Freud's early patients, and he wrote to ask if I would consider giving him access to the various historical materials I have collected from my many years' research into the early years of psychoanalysis. So I wrote back saying I would gladly coöperate—so long as he would reciprocate by granting me access to the biographical information on Fliess.

In their early correspondence, in the winter and spring of 1980, Swales and Masson were like two dogs sniffing at each other. Masson, writing from Munich, where he had gone to study German, wanted to know "How did you come to work on the early Freud? Are you an analyst? Did you do formal studies in the history of science or psychology?

Is your German fluent? How did you get in touch with Freud's early patients?" Swales replied, "I am not an analyst—nor have I ever undergone a psychoanalysis. In fact, I am not even a man of science. As one whose *akademische Laufbahn* jumped the rails at the age of sixteen, I do not even have a higher education. I fear by temperament I am little more than an adventurer. Such persons are apt to be cherished if they succeed, if they really discover something; otherwise, they are cast by the wayside." (Swales was here making a knowing allusion to a letter to Fliess, quoted by Jones, in which Freud says of himself, "I am not really a man of science, not an observer, not an experimenter, and not a thinker. I am nothing but by temperament a *conquistador*—an adventurer, if you want to translate the word—with the curiosity, the boldness, and the tenacity that belong to that type of being. Such people are apt to be treasured if they succeed, if they have really discovered something; otherwise, they are thrown aside.") Swales went on to offer a proposal: "Frankly—if I may venture to make such a statement as a matter of fact rather than of immodesty—my knowledge of Freud's life and work during the formative Fliess years is, historically speaking, so enormous that I think it would make sense if you were to give serious consideration to the idea of enlisting my aid in annotating and introducing the letters to Fliess. But since I am absolutely independent and have no outside funding to speak of, for that I would require a fee." "I am afraid that is impossible," Masson quickly replied, "since my contract is already signed and makes me solely responsible for the new edition. . . . As for money, alas, I have none. I am myself Professor of Sanskrit at the University of Toronto, and I have felt obliged to stop my analytic practice in order to devote myself full time to these letters." "In my last letter I was not trying to gate-crash your work in the sense of demanding a formal collaboration!" Swales protested. "I simply wanted to have the opportunity—given appropriate credit, of course—to contribute to your endeavor all that important information and material which I am personally responsible for having brought to light." He went on to propose that Masson raise four thousand dollars "in order that you, my wife, who is my translator, and I could undertake two separate trips together so that I may personally introduce you to the mass of stuff I have located on Fliess." Swales was here alluding to the Jerusalem *Nachlass,* which he did not yet trust Masson enough to mention by name. Then, like a salesman slowly opening his sample case to a housewife softened up by the pitch, he proceeded to display one tantalizing example after another of his research into the life of Fliess and Freud. Masson took the bait. "Your work is marvellous!" he wrote back. "You have been able to do what many people with all possible underwriting have been unable to even get close to. . . . You have indeed shown me how essential your work is for mine. . . . But now you must help me find a solution so that both of us are not held up in our work. Because, even though you have done by far the greater amount of research and have much to offer the new edition, I also have material to which there is no possible way you could gain access without my help. Namely, the unpublished Fliess letters, in the first rank, but also several hundred unpublished letters of Freud to which only I have been granted access. I am perfectly prepared to give you access to this material in return for the same courtesy on your part."

On hearing this, Swales hesitated no longer about revealing the Jerusalem *Nachlass.* ("You cannot hold it against a man for declining to play all his cards at once," he wrote Masson in explanation of his earlier guardedness. "Sometimes it is important to keep a few trumps up one's sleeve.") He again asked Masson to raise the money for the trip to Israel, which again Masson declined to do. "We have both decided to dedicate our life to scholarship, and certain sacrifices must be made," Masson piously wrote on April 21, 1980, adding, "I was delighted to learn that Dr. Eissler was able to get you a grant, and now I find, to my pleasure, that he thinks he will be able to help me as well! We are both lucky to have such an understanding, distinguished, and powerful friend."

Four days earlier, Eissler had written Masson asking him to be his successor at the Archives, and two weeks later Masson flew home to Berkeley, stopping off in New York for two days, to see Eissler. During Masson's stay in New York (at the Eissler apartment), Eissler brought his two protégés together at a Sunday brunch, at which his wife was also present. Swales concluded a ten-page handwritten account of the meeting (it is his habit to record all conversations of any substance directly after they have taken place) with the comment "Masson struck me as the wrong man for the job: insufficient background; biassed views; too hasty and impulsive in decision; and he doesn't listen (therefore learn) properly. He's a novice in the field of historical research." But Swales had already formed a poor opinion of Masson, from his letters. "Nobody in my world of correspondence—historians, scholars, professors—wrote letters so scatterbrained and impulsive," he told me. "That alerted me about him; it put me off. The clumsy, bungled syntax, the misspellings, and so on. I go through my letters with a fine-tooth comb, so to speak. I couldn't live with a misspelling or bad grammar. My pride wouldn't allow that." Swales went on to say that the brunch started off in what was, for him, an alarming way. "When I arrived, I could see that they had been talking about me. They asked me questions that had a premeditated ring to them. And the very first question they asked me—it came out of Masson's mouth, with a little elaboration from Eissler—was 'Do you believe that Freud and his sister-in-law had a love affair?' I secretly gulped. I thought, My God, they know! But I composed myself in a flash and said, 'Well, I must be absolutely frank with you. I have very good reason to believe not only that they did have an affair but that Minna exerted a very strong influence on Freud's work.' To my amazement, they didn't freak out or anything. Eissler said to me, in his challenging way, 'How do you know this? How can you say that?' So I launched into an encapsulated version of what, eighteen months later, was to become my lecture on Freud's affair with Minna. As I did this, Masson kept derailing the conversation. I thought to myself, Why did the idiot ask me the question if he doesn't want to listen to the answer? It went on like this, and before I knew it the conversation about Freud and Minna had been dropped. Masson kept talking this ridiculous nonsense. It got to the point where Eissler got furious with him and said, 'Professor Masson, would you be quiet and let Mr. Swales talk?' They were very flattering to me. They asked me to use my 'brilliant detective skills' to track down a missing letter of Freud to Fliess, and called me a 'genius,' and 'Sherlock Holmes,' and things like that. As I was leaving, Masson dumped a typewriter on me—a big German machine he had bought in Germany and didn't want to drag on the plane to California. I already had three typewriters, but, all right, this one had umlauts, so I accepted it." (I later heard from Masson his version of the typewriter incident: "All through the brunch, Swales kept eyeing the typewriter longingly, so finally, in a burst of generosity, I gave it to him. He was this poor guy who had nothing—no money, his wife had to bake cookies, he didn't have a typewriter, he didn't even have paper to write on, he was uneducated, his research methods were primitive, he had no knowledge of languages, he didn't read a single word of French—and I had a certain sympathy for him. He reminded me of myself when I first arrived at Harvard. But I guess I mainly wanted to show Eissler that I wasn't an envious, malicious, backbiting sort of person—that here was somebody young and not particularly illustrious I could be nice to. I gave the typewriter to Swales very ostentatiously in front of the Eisslers to show them how generous I could be, and it felt good when Eissler turned to his wife and gave her a meaningful look: See what a nice gesture!")

Swales continued, "I had met with Eissler several times by this time, and I was fascinated with him as a person. I liked him a lot. A funny thing had happened at our third meeting. He had already promised me the grant. He said to me, 'Mr. Swales, I don't know that you're not a rascal. How do I know that you won't go and publish nasty things about Freud?' And I paused and said, 'Well, Dr. Eissler, I can't sit here and defend myself. If I start defending myself against something like that, it's going to sound as if I had something to hide. It's up to you to make of me what you can. Here I am. You can see what my work is. I go off, I find documents, I come up with the goods. Draw your own conclusions.'

"At the brunch, I had to face up to the moral dimension of my situation. There I was, infiltrating the sanctum sanctorum, the holy of holies, the Freud Archives. Where did that put me? I thought, That's what journalists do, that's what spies do—which triggered a whole romantic dimension that I'm not indifferent to. But on the other hand, I thought, they're getting material from me, so if I take material from them I'm entitled to it, I've earned the right to it. Their material shouldn't even be bloody locked up. I thought I could break the Freud Archives' monopoly on material, because I was the only person to come along who had amassed not a competitive amount of material—that would be ridiculous to claim—but certainly crucial material.

"In Masson I immediately recognized a kind of mirror image of a part of myself. He is an entrepreneur, a hustler. I had been involved in hyping rock music. I had always been in business. I had gravitated toward New York City for that reason—it's the mecca of hype and business and bullshit. Then, eight years ago, I went through a spiritual and moral crisis: I was confronted with the question, Do I want to spend the rest of my life bullshitting away like all those hacks and hype artists, or do I want to do something of value? I came out of the crisis with the decision to work on Freud and to do it well."

Swales somewhat hesitantly told me of the influence on his life of Georges Ivanovich Gurdjiev, the Russian mystic/teacher/psychologist who came into prominence in France between the wars (and died in Paris in 1949), and of whom Swales has been a follower since the age of nineteen. "I feel it will make you very unsympathetic toward me if I discuss Gurdjiev any further," Swales said. "As far as I'm concerned, Gurdjiev is the most profound psychological genius who ever trod this earth. But it would be pointless to talk about him in any specific way. When I was younger, I made the mistake of referring people to his books. I no longer do that. To understand Gurdjiev, one would have to participate in what is called the Gurdjiev 'work'—learn the Gurdjiev dances, grasp certain concepts, expose oneself to certain experiences. It would be pointless to try to explain it to an outsider."

After the Eissler brunch, Swales began storing up grievances against Masson. He said nothing to Masson, silently permitting his anger, resentment, dislike, and envy to build up to the explosion point. When the explosion came, a year later, in the spring of 1981, it was set off, oddly, not by any action of Masson's but by a paper he wrote entitled "Freud and 19th-Century Psychiatry," of which he had sent Swales a copy. This paper so incensed Swales ("It is a disgusting piece of scribble," Swales wrote in the forty-five-page letter. "I find it a travesty, an absolute disgrace to Freud scholarship. . . . All in all, I think it is about the worst piece of writing on Freud I have ever had the displeasure to read —and that is really saying something") that he felt he had to go to Eissler and lay before him his case against Masson.*

* Swales did not spell out to Eissler his chief objection to the paper on nineteenth-century psychiatry—namely, its uneasy but as yet undeviating pro-Freudian stance. But to Masson, he wrote, "You are constantly accusing the parents and the authorities of Freud's day of being evil and sadistic—as if Freud was himself totally removed from this Zeitgeist. Yet Freud is notorious for having, with *his* theories of human development, copped out of that problem; he effectively incriminated the *children* rather than the parents, burdening the former with the onus of their later (adult) psychopathology. . . . It really must be some perverted twist of fate that you are in such reverence of Freud, rather than, say, of Otto Gross, or even Wilhelm Reich. . . .

"Without mincing my words, I proceeded to complain about your competence, conduct, and integrity," Swales recalled in the letter to Masson, and he continued:

> Eissler gave me a fair enough hearing, I suppose. But he took issue with me on many points along the way, and in such a manner that after a while it became clear to me that our conversation was doomed to be futile. In short, while attempting to fault me in certain details, Dr. Eissler showed himself to be very reluctant to look at the whole picture I was striving to convey. Dr. Eissler recommended that I address all my criticisms directly to you. He claimed that you were very open to criticism. Nevertheless—in response to my complaint that you just do not know how to shut up and listen when someone happens to be speaking on a matter with far greater authority than you could muster, and that therefore you render yourself virtually incapable of learning anything new, even when it might be vitally in your own interests that you do so— he argued that I would just have to face that, that nothing would ever change you, that you just never stop talking, and that this is your nature.

"I knew I was burning my bridges when I went to Eissler to complain about Masson," Swales told me. "I knew he would go to all kinds of lengths to defend his *goldenes Kind,* and that he would hold it against me. But I had to do it."

On April 5, 1981, the day after the visit to Eissler, Swales and Masson spoke together on the telephone, for the last time. The conversation flared into a bitter quarrel, and Masson proposed that they break off relations. Swales counterproposed that they talk together again in June, when Masson

would be in New York, but Masson said no, and he later
wrote a note to Swales curtly terminating their association.

In the forty-five-page letter, written eleven days after the
quarrel on the telephone, Swales sets down his grievances
against Masson in what he calls "the most extensive—albeit
perhaps, if necessary, the most tedious and boring—manner,"
adding, "Understand that here I am not concerned to write
any kind of a literary presentation. Rather, I am writing for
the benefit of the historical record." But the letter is nothing
if not a literary presentation. To sustain the reader's interest
in an endless diatribe against someone whose sins have
largely been those of careless and thoughtless omission
(Masson did not send Swales the material he had promised,
he ignored his questions, he did not help him raise money
for the trip to Israel, he did not try to get him appointed to
the Board of the Archives, he did not treat him with respect,
he simply didn't bother very much about him) requires literary skill not often given to the writers of angry screeds. But,
astonishingly, Swales's screed is unfailingly interesting. In
Henry James's phrase, Swales is "one of the people on whom
nothing is lost," and, like a James character, he takes things
very far. Just as it is possible to look up from a James novel
and suddenly wonder whether all these people aren't completely crazy (in James's late novel *The Sacred Fount,* he
himself actually puts this subversive idea into the mouth of
a character), so it occasionally occurs to the reader of Swales's
letter to wonder about the sanity of a man who composes a
recitation of his injuries that is as long as a novella. But the
narrative sweep, the energy, the intelligence, and the high
spirits of Swales's writing outweigh the triviality of much of
what he says and the lunacy of the lengths to which he goes
to say it. When Swales finished the letter (it took him three

days to write), he felt triumphant. He went out and had several dozen Xeroxes made, and after sending Masson, Eissler, and the other regulars on his mailing list their copies, he bestowed copies on whoever came along in the next few weeks. One of these recipients was the revisionist psychoanalyst Milton Klein, who happened to stop into the small office on Mott Street that Swales had rented for his Freud and Fliess work. After reading the letter, Klein passed it on to his colleague and collaborator David Tribich, with whom he was writing a book on Freud's seduction theory. Tribich then passed it on to his brother-in-law Ralph Blumenthal. On July 1, 1981, Tribich wrote to Swales, who was then doing research in Vienna, on a second-year grant from the New-Land Foundation:

Dear Peter:

I'm not sure you know my name, but I am Milton Klein's friend and colleague.

I mentioned to Milton some weeks ago that you might be interested in publicizing in the N.Y. *Times* your dispute with Masson and his reneging on his agreement with you. I'm in full sympathy with you in this matter. When Milton told me you were very interested, I mentioned it to my wife's brother, Ralph Blumenthal— a reporter for the *Times*. As it turns out, the *Times* editors are greatly interested in covering this, and although I said you were in Europe for the summer, they wanted to reach you immediately.

Best regards,

David Tribich

By the time Swales received Tribich's letter, he had already heard from Blumenthal, who telephoned him from

New York on July 1 and proposed to fly to Vienna on July 11 and meet Swales in the well-known café called Demel's. A few days later, Blumenthal telephoned again, to make final arrangements. He brought up Swales's theory about Minna and Freud and the story about Freud's "plot" to murder Fliess—which had been mentioned in the forty-five-page letter—but Swales refused to speak about these two subjects. "I told Blumenthal, 'I can't talk to you about Minna and the plot to murder Fliess, because I'm under contract to the London *Sunday Times* about that,'" Swales said to me. "Blumenthal said, 'But, Peter, if you won't talk there's not much point in my coming to Vienna.' I said, 'I guess there isn't.' Blumenthal said, 'If you won't talk to me, I'll have to go talk to Masson.' I said, 'You do what you like.' And in that moment I saw what was going to happen. Blumenthal had had the idea that Klein was an authority on what was happening in psychoanalysis, and so he had let Klein steer him toward the seduction theory as the center of his article. I knew that Masson wouldn't be able to keep his mouth shut. Ralph Blumenthal, being a newspaper reporter, is skilled at getting people to talk, and I knew Masson would succumb to Blumenthal's flattery. So Masson, in turn, was steered by Blumenthal to blab about the seduction theory, and my story got lost and buried, and I was thankful. I had known that Masson would sooner or later put his foot in it. I didn't know how, but I knew the guy's got to blunder badly and get booted out, one way or another. When Blumenthal said, 'I'll go talk to Masson,' I more or less knew how the rest of the scenario would go. I knew that Masson would shoot his mouth off and that Eissler would finally have to face the truth about him."

2

IsN'T Freud an interesting, fascinating personality? I don't know what is so unusual in my admiration for him. His language, his thoughts! His dream book is really an outstanding feat. Do I overrate Freud?" Eissler sat facing me at his desk during one of our evening conversations, speaking with his usual asperity.

I said, "Nobody writes about Freud the way you do. Nobody has the feeling for him that you have." I was thinking of Eissler's essay on Freud's personal letters, "Mankind at Its Best," which is almost embarrassingly rhapsodic. Almost. In the end, Eissler somehow manages to erode the reader's resistance to his thesis that Freud was a near-perfect man, and when one rereads the letters themselves (they were collected by Freud's son Ernst in 1960), they have been changed by Eissler's passionate involvement with them, and have taken on a lustre—the way someone we have met casually, and who has not fascinated us, becomes suddenly interesting when a mutual friend praises him extravagantly.

"Tell me about this feeling," Eissler said. "I mean, do I use excessive terms? In reconstructing what went on with Freud, do I exaggerate? Do I not produce enough documents to justify my conclusions? I know I have this reputation about Freud, and I have come to see that there is no sense fighting it. I don't even discuss Freud with my colleagues anymore, because they laugh when I start. A few years ago, a colleague at the Psychoanalytic Institute read a paper on Freud, and when he was finished I got up and said, 'There are nine mistakes,' and—laughter. They take it as a foregone conclusion that I will defend Freud. But I don't think I am uncritical. In *Talent and Genius,* I describe Freud's headaches—they were neurotic symptoms, no doubt—his digestive difficulties, his migraines, his compulsions. But it doesn't amount to much. That is the strange thing." The door of Eissler's consultation room suddenly opened and a large dog walked in. He came over and sniffed me in a friendly but unintrusive way, and then trotted over to the analytic couch, jumped up on it, pawed at the blanket that lay folded at the foot until it looked like an unmade bed, and lay down and went to sleep. "Whenever somebody writes something against Freud, it is accepted almost with pleasure," Eissler went on. "No one is interested if you write positively about Freud, but as soon as you write negatively everybody applauds. The people who write against Freud are motivated by a desire for revenge. Freud hurt us—he hurt all of us deeply by his findings—and now there is an attempt to get back at him through denigration of his character. Imagine! Swales 'proves' that Freud seriously planned to kill Fliess! Every time I read one of these 'revelations,' I think the bottom has been reached. Roazen writes that Freud was responsible for Tausk's suicide. Krüll writes that Freud watched his father masturbate and suppressed the seduction theory in order to protect him. Masson writes that Freud dropped the seduction theory out of cowardice and to further his career. Each time something is released by Anna Freud or the Archives, these things are written."

I said, "You had no suspicion that Masson might come out against Freud?"

"Not a bit. He was always full of praise for Freud, for me, for Anna Freud. He was extreme in his criticism of anybody who criticized Freud. He was against Krüll, Kohut, Erikson, Roazen, Sulloway—anybody who ever said anything against Freud."

"He argues that he was always very open about his views, that everyone always knew what they were, and that he was fired only because he aired them in a newspaper," I said.

"The manuscripts he sent me I did not read very carefully," Eissler admitted. "I relied on him. Why should I go so carefully through those manuscripts? They were pretty long, I had very much to do, my eyesight is bad and I don't read very well—so I just glanced over them. I didn't find anything obnoxious. If I look at it analytically, it was probably because I did not want to read them. When, finally, I did read his New Haven paper carefully, I found it quite objectionable." Eissler showed me a testy critique of the paper he had sent his protégé on September 25, 1981. It read, in part:

You say it was quite obscure why Freud dropped the seduction theory. Well, only when an author replaces a correct theory with an erroneous one is it possible to raise such a question. Is it so surprising that Freud discovered a wrong theory to be wrong?

You claim that Freud dropped the seduction theory because Krafft-Ebing and the rest of the audience [of Freud's "Aetiology of Hysteria" paper] rejected it. This is quite impossible, because the new theory, which he published in 1905, got him in even greater trouble and disrepute than the theory of 1895. Thus, your reasoning makes no sense. In addition, when you say that it was for the sake of quasi-ingratiating himself with authority that he dropped the seduction theory, the reader must conclude that the seduction theory was correct, and that Freud dropped it for unscientific reasons. I do hope that you do not plan to write such things in your introduction to the Freud-Fliess letters. You propose here—without documentation—the existence of a trait in Freud's character which implies a grave accusation against his reliability, honesty, and solidity. Not even his worst enemies have ever claimed that he evolved theories in order to make his person acceptable to the academic community. If you want to escape criticism, you have to present solid and convincing documentation.

The conversation turned to Swales. "He knew more than Masson," Eissler said. "He was very skillful at finding documents. He had this uncanny flair for knowing where to go, and he had a wonderful memory. I was impressed that he was a pure idealist. He had no money. He lived a very destitute life, so I got him a grant through the Archives. How stupid I was! Whenever I became pessimistic, I would think, Look at Masson and Swales, two idealists, the one giving up his academic career, the other living in great poverty and devoting himself to finding documents about Freud —isn't that really touching? Swales seemed so disarming, charming, naïve. My goodness, I thought, I would like to give him ten dollars and do something for him."

I repeated to Eissler a comment Swales had made to me —a complaint that locking up material in the Archives for a hundred years favored the unborn and discriminated against scholars working today.

"I could tell him of far greater injustices—the unequal distribution of wealth, the killing of innocent people," Eissler retorted, with bland irrelevance.

"Do you feel that people living in the next century will be in a better position to write about Freud?"

"They will have more distance. They will be more objective. I hope they will be free of Swales's prejudices. Injustice! I think it is a far greater injustice that Swales may publish whatever he wants about Freud, and that Freud cannot defend himself and prove he is being maligned."

3

I HAVE a card that says 'Resident Alien'—that describes me," Peter Swales told me during one of our afternoon talks. "A guy like me is inevitably interested in drugs, sex, rock and roll, Jews, psychopathology, the history of religion. Certain subjects naturally fall into my lap because they're borderline subjects. I am profoundly a misfit in the modern world, in terms of what the modern world wants from you: to work for a bank or a company, to have some defined specialist function. When I was a kid, I had the problem of being small. I couldn't compete on a physical level—God hadn't given me big muscles and a big body to avoid being bullied—so I had to find some other way of protecting myself. I found it through manipulating people, through using words, through thinking things out. For instance, there was a trick I learned when I was at school: never lead boys. There's always some boy who stands up and wants to be the leader. But in history leaders get their heads chopped off, they get put down, they lose their crowns —so I'd always become *second* to the leader. I'd win influence over him, and have him act on my suggestions. But when he fell I would be in the clear, and would go and attach myself to the next leader. I was always trying to out-manipulate everyone—my folks, my teachers, my friends.

"When I had my spiritual crisis eight years ago, which ended with the decision to devote myself to Freud scholarship, I was sick of myself. I didn't like Peter Swales at all. The way I treated my wife disgusted me—always manipulating, never really being able to be forthright. The hype artist in me couldn't stop. He was running amok. I could see it. I didn't want to live like that. I didn't want to die like that. And in taking on Freud I was taking on the monster that existed in myself. When I came to Freud, when I looked at the man, I immediately knew who he was. When I read *The Interpretation of Dreams,* I recognized the web of deception he was weaving. The way Freud's mind worked was totally familiar to me. I knew the games he was playing, I was totally versed in his manipulative logic and rhetoric. And I knew there was a man hiding behind a mask—it didn't add up otherwise. For instance, a man cannot write about sexuality the way Freud does and be so dispassionate toward it. And then when I read the Fliess letters and compared the man in them to the man in the Jones biography I knew I was on the right track. I don't think Eissler could ever understand Freud. Freud is much too complex, devious, sinister a man for Eissler. I'll tell you quite honestly, I'm the only person who has ever really understood Freud. I'm not asking you to believe that—you can judge for yourself—but leave it till you read my essay on Minna Bernays.

"My starting point is that all people are devious and sinister, that they're shits. For me, the world is full of shit, so I'm not disappointed. Now, you could retort, 'Well, then, how did you get into such a situation with Jeffrey Masson?' And that's where all my philosophy of life falls flat. Because a guy like me—well, beggars can't be choosers. Masson and the Archives had something I wanted, and I had to go along on their terms. Likewise, if you're not in a strong financial situation in life, then it's difficult, because you're always trying to pull yourself up by your shoestrings. You allow yourself to get into situations you wouldn't get into if you had money. I'm constantly being deceived and betrayed by the Massons of the world. Yes, there have been others. There is a man in England named Oliver Gillie, a journalist, by whom I was also wickedly betrayed."

In October 1976, Oliver Gillie, the medical correspondent of the London *Sunday Times,* published an article in that paper about the fraudulent research of Cyril Burt, who had faked data to support his theories about the heritability of intelligence. Swales telephoned Gillie and told him he had evidence of similar "deceptions" on the part of Sigmund Freud; would Gillie be interested in writing an article based on Swales's research? Gillie was interested, and a contract was duly drawn up between Swales and the *Sunday Times,* giving Swales a thousand pounds for material he would supply in the form of two essays, out of which Gillie would create a feature article. ("I approached Gillie," Swales told me, "because I was back at my parents' house, doing the prodigal-son number and living at their expense, and I was desperate to show them a promissory note, so they'd know that I wasn't just messing around.") The arrangement seemed straightforward enough—but four years and hundreds of pages of correspondence later, the article had still not appeared, and Gillie and Swales were locked in a stranglehold from which neither seemed able to extricate himself. Swales had been unable to simply give the *Sunday Times* his essays and let Gillie write his piece, and Gillie, for his part, had been unable to resist Swales's fatal "help," so that the most hopelessly tangled and mired situation developed between the two men. Swales would send Gillie new essays, which Gillie would rework into a new two-part article, which Swales would inveigh against in his customary long letters. Finally, in the summer of 1981, after receiving a ten-page letter of protest from Swales about Gillie's latest version ("Were you to print the articles, quite frankly, I think I would abandon all my work on Freud and take a straight job, so sour would the whole thing have become for me," Swales wrote. "Of course, I do not want that to happen, so, as far as I am concerned, not to mince words, I think the best thing you can do is stick those articles up your fucking arses. That is all they are good for. They are a travesty of my work and of Freud history"), the *Sunday Times* had had enough. "I have consulted Eric Jacobs [a colleague] on the subject of your letter," Lewis Chester, the *Sunday Times*'s special features editor, wrote to Swales on August 19, "and he and I are agreed that there is no point in wasting any more money or man-hours on your Freud material. On a more personal note, I would like to say how delighted I am not to have made your acquaintance." Then, in December 1981, to Swales's horror and dismay, the *Sunday Times* decided to print the articles after all—the first under the heading "Sex and Cocaine: Freud's Pact with the Devil," and the second as "The Secret Love Life of Sigmund Freud." Swales tried to enlist the British Law Society in filing a suit against the *Sunday Times,* but was refused. He looks back on his involvement with Gillie as an unmitigated disaster; like his involvement with Masson, he views it as a product of his "weak position in life."

Over tea, Swales went on to tell me that he had known from the start that he could never win the place in Eissler's affections that Masson held. "I could never have had that kind of relationship with him," he said. "Eissler would never have 'adopted' me the way he adopted Masson. I didn't have that kind of personality. I wasn't Jewish. There was always a distance between me and Eissler." When the story of Masson's firing from the Archives broke, Swales wrote to Eissler, humorously offering to take Masson's place:

> Dear Dr. Eissler,
>
> When I saw you quoted this morning in the New York *Times* dismissing the work of Masson as "plain nonsense," I felt tempted for a moment to take out a plagiarism suit against you. But I decided to refrain from any action and ask you instead for proper attribution in future.
>
> Now that you have dispatched that Alberich to Hades, may I offer my own services as replacement? I would happily settle for a mere 33% of his annual salary —i.e. $10,000 p.a.—and I can assure you I would do the job 2,467 times better.

Eissler wrote back saying, "Thank you for offering your good services for an annual salary of $10,000. I will submit your offer to the Board of the Archives at our next meeting" —which was the end of that, since the next scheduled Board meeting was eleven months away. But if Eissler had accepted his half-serious offer, "I would have worked faithfully as archivist for him for ten years," Swales said. "I would have been willing to put off doing my own work for the privilege of being around Eissler, of learning from him."

In his letter offering his services, Swales also urged Eissler "to make every effort to attend my lecture at N.Y.U. on November 18th," adding, "Many people of eminence in Freud scholarship plan to be there, and—dare I say it—the lecture already seems destined to become an historic occasion in the history of psychoanalytic scholarship." When Swales wrote these brave words, he had not yet written his lecture. Then, five days before the date, "I drank a whole bottle of wine and wrote it all in one night," he told me. "It just came out like that, because I was that well rehearsed in the data." This was the first time Swales had spoken in public, and when he sat down, after nearly three hours of speaking, he received a standing ovation from the audience of psychologists, psychiatrists, analysts, and academics. In the lecture, he offered his thesis that Freud and Minna Bernays had been lovers, that during a trip to Italy he had made her pregnant, and that he had then arranged for her to have an abortion, under the cover of taking her to a spa for the treatment of tuberculosis. The lecture (which has since been published in the journal *The New American Review*) is a dazzling tour de force. For evidence of the affair and the abortion, Swales goes to Freud's own writings; the centerpiece of his argument is a noted passage in *The Psychopathology of Everyday Life,* known as the Aliquis analysis, in which Freud asks a young man he has met on a holiday trip to associate to a word the young man had unaccountably been unable to recall while quoting a well-known line from Virgil: *"Ex-*

oriare aliquis nostris ex ossibus ultor." The young man's associations to *"aliquis"* presently lead him to an embarrassing thought. Freud writes:

"Well, go on. Why do you pause?"

"Well, something *has* come into my mind . . . but it's too intimate to pass on. . . . Besides, I don't see any connection, or any necessity for saying it."

"You can leave the connection to me. Of course, I can't force you to talk about something that you find distasteful; but then you mustn't insist on learning from me how you came to forget your *'aliquis.'* "

"Really? Is that what you think? Well, then, I've suddenly thought of a lady from whom I might easily hear a piece of news that would be very awkward for both of us."

"That her periods have stopped?"

"How could you guess that?"

"That's not difficult any longer; you've prepared the way sufficiently. Think of the calendar saints, the blood that starts to flow on a particular day, the disturbance when the event fails to take place, the open threats that the miracle must be vouchsafed, or else. . . . In fact, you've made use of the miracle of St. Januarius to manufacture a brilliant allusion to women's periods."

"Without being aware of it. And you really mean to say that it was this anxious expectation that made me unable to produce an unimportant word like *'aliquis'?* "

"It seems to me undeniable. You need only recall the division you made into *'a-liquis,'* and your associations: relics, liquefying, fluid. St. Simon was sacrificed as a child —shall I go on and show how he comes in? You were led on to him by the subject of relics."

"No, I'd much rather you didn't. I hope you don't take these thoughts of mine too seriously, if indeed I really had them. In return, I will confess to you that the lady is Italian, in whose company I also visited Naples."

Swales's argument—that the man who had forgotten *"aliquis"* was Freud himself, covertly speaking of his own situation with Minna—is so cogently developed and so firmly grounded in the biographical actuality that Swales established during the seven years of his Freud research that it is practically impossible to refute. The whole thing is immensely satisfying to contemplate as a piece of intellectual work; there are no loose ends, all the pieces fit, the joints are elegant. But it's all wrong. It's like a Van Meegeren forgery of Vermeer, in which all the pieces fit, too, but from which the soul of the original is entirely, almost absurdly, missing. It is possible (though unlikely) that Freud had an affair with his sister-in-law, who came to live in the Freud household after the death of her fiancé and remained for forty years. (The rumor of an affair was spread by Carl Jung, who told an interviewer in 1957 that Minna had confided the secret to him; Freudians have dismissed Jung's revelation as a malicious lie, while anti-Freudians have been inclined to give it credence.) But if Freud had had the misfortune to fall in love with his wife's sister, *and* to make her pregnant, *and* to have to get her an abortion, is it probable, psychologically speaking, that he would have sat down a few months later and cheerfully worked these miserable and sordid events into his clever and lighthearted Aliquis analysis? How callous can a man get? It was on this point—on its psychological improbability—rather than on some of the questions of factual detail raised by Freud scholars, that I found I couldn't accept Swales's reconstruction, however greatly I relished its elaboration.

Eissler, as one might expect, couldn't accept it, either. Although he didn't attend the lecture, he heard about it from colleagues and read about it in the *Times*. (The faithful Blumenthal had written about it in the *Times* of November 22, in a story captioned "Historian Links Freud and Wife's Sister as Lovers.") On January 10, 1982, Swales wrote to Eissler, "The other day, I was told that you are highly skeptical of the thesis I put forward in my lecture at N.Y.U. in November, and that you characterize the whole business as being merely 'rumors' about Freud's sex life. But I urge you, Dr. Eissler, not to take up an untenable position against me in that regard. The general verdict among those who attended the lecture is that it was one of outstanding scholarship, and that my historical reconstruction is far more soundly founded than Freudian reconstructions. If you would like a transcript of the lecture for your private perusal, then please let me know, as I will be only too happy to oblige." Eissler wrote back, "I am touched by your concern about my salvation. If you wish to donate a transcript of your lecture to the Sigmund Freud Archives, it will certainly be accepted and forwarded to the Library of Congress. If I find time to read it, I will be glad to do so. Depending on what you wrote, I might publish a rebuttal. If you do not desire the latter, please let me know in time."

On March 11, Swales wrote Eissler a letter that ranks with the forty-five-page letter to Masson in its biliousness, if not in its length (a mere twelve pages). As Swales had foreseen, relations between him and Eissler deteriorated after he went to Eissler to complain about Masson. Eissler's only response to the forty-five-page letter had been to ask Swales to send proof that Masson had offered to let Swales see unpublished material. When Swales sent the damning letters, Eissler didn't respond; he dropped Swales as abruptly and as impulsively as he had picked him up and showered him with money and flattering attention—just as, with infinitely more regret, he was to drop the irrepressible Masson.

Human nature is such that when we are suddenly taken up by someone whom we consider superior and admirable, we accept his attentions calmly, whereas when we are dropped we cannot rest until we feel we have got to the bottom of the person's profound irrationality. Nor can we easily accept the verdict sent down to us through the mortifying silence of someone who has found us wanting and has packed up and moved on. We protest it, each in our way—our futile way, since the more effective is our protest the more surely do we drive away the person whose love we have lost not because of anything we did, but because of who we are. By protesting Eissler's withdrawal from him with an outrageous lawsuit, Masson only confirmed Eissler in his appalled recognition of who his protégé was. By sending Eissler an outrageous letter (in which he had the impudence to refer to Anna Freud as "the Blessed Virgin of psychoanalysis"), Swales only impelled his former benefactor to retreat further and further from him. Swales had heard from his former associate Robert Byck, among others, that Eissler had called him "schizophrenic" and "paranoid," and in his letter he demanded of Eissler that he "hasten to write me apologizing for having denounced me as 'schizophrenic' and 'paranoid,'" and he went on, "You will also send copies of your letter to all those to whom you have said such things—or you will supply me with all their names and addresses so I can do the job for you. If, however, you stand by what you have said about me, then I must urge you to be man enough to *publish* such views—in which case I may seek to litigate the matter in a court of law." Swales sustained this dire tone in eleven of the twelve pages (several were occupied with a bellicose defense of the Minna Bernays thesis), and then, in the final paragraph, he made a surprising about-face:

> Having fired away like this, now I would just like to say how sorry I am, how deeply I regret the fact that this letter is so brutal. Were it not that you would certainly distrust my motives, having now said what I have, I would like to be able to say, Can't we make up and be friends? Let me tell you, even if you were "hung, drawn, and quartered" I would still like you.* More than that, though, I think you are a great polemicist and a talented thinker, albeit at times a deluded one. Isn't it a shame that our common preoccupation with Freud should drive up apart rather than bring us together? I think that this must say something awfully significant about Freud, rather than anything very much about you or me. Let me repeat, then, I really like you, and while I am ready to do battle if need be right up to the hilt, it causes me great personal sorrow that we are at war. We could be learning oh, so very much from one another.

* Swales is here alluding to a letter that Eissler once sent to Milton Klein. A hypnotist named Milton V. Kline, who had testified as an expert witness on behalf of John Lennon's killer and also of the man accused (and ultimately acquitted) of pushing Renée Katz in the path of a subway train, had just pleaded guilty to lying under oath about his professional credentials. Eissler, who had recently become friendly with the innocent Klein, wrote to inquire if he was the guilty Kline, adding, "Even if you were hung, drawn, and quartered, I would still like you." Klein eventually went the way of so many of Eissler's enthusiasms: he incurred Eissler's displeasure with a paper called "On Freud's 'Blindness.'"

In his reply, Eissler passed over Swales's overture in silence, merely saying, with unaccustomed prudence, "In reviewing the observations which gave me the feeling that you suffer from schizophrenia, I realize that this impression was wrong. I therefore retract the statement I made to Professor Byck and apologize for having made it."

Eissler's diagnosis of Swales as a schizophrenic cut deep, and continues to rankle. "If you've ever met a schizophrenic, there's no way that you could properly call me schizophrenic," Swales told me one afternoon indignantly. But on other occasions he would say, with a mischievous smile, "Maybe Eissler is right. Maybe I am schizophrenic." One afternoon, he said, "Let me tell you of an episode of clinical paranoia I once went through. It happened in 1969, while I was working for the Rolling Stones. I was racked by toothache and was doped up on codeine, taking twelve to thirteen tablets a day. The Stones had given a Saturday-afternoon concert in Hyde Park, and after the concert I stayed behind in the park. I was sitting in a deck chair by the Serpentine, near a copse that has a high metal fence around it, and I saw this guy coming toward me. I looked at this man, and in a moment of superior intuition I read everything about him—his body posture, the way he came across—and it all added up to me that he had something to hide. Everything about him exuded something strange, hidden, guilty. And he was looking into the copse as he walked past it. This is where the delusion comes in. I thought, Why is he so interested in the copse? And then I thought—it's mind-boggling to reflect on it now—I thought, Wow! This man is a spy! I should explain that there was a roadway that went into the copse through a big gate, and standing in front of this gate was a park attendant, maybe even a security guard. So I immediately leaped to the conclusion that in this copse in the middle of Hyde Park in London there was a British Intelligence center. There's some logic to this conclusion, because adjacent to Hyde Park are the royal residences of Princess Margaret and the Queen Mother, and also the Russian Embassy and the Czechoslovak Embassy and all those other Communist embassies, and I thought, It's obvious: we're picking up signals from all these embassies, and this guy is a Communist spy. He walked around the fence, and I followed him to see what he was doing. He was wearing the classic clothes of a spy—an old raincoat—and every step he took confirmed me in my belief that he was an espionage agent. So I thought, Wow! I'll track him, prove that he's a spy, and become famous overnight for catching a spy. He began to realize that he was being trailed, and there followed a half-hour scene that is classic in the movies, with him hiding behind trees and looking out, and me getting out from behind my tree and following. We went around the copse in this way once or twice, whereupon he shifts into a very brisk pace, walks out of the park, and starts to go up this street called Kensington Palace Gardens, with me in pursuit. Now, wait for this: I run up to a cop in Kensington Palace Gardens— this is where all the embassies are—and point at the guy and say, 'Look, Officer, he's a spy! You must arrest him!' The cop looks at me like I'm daft, and says, 'What makes you believe that?' and I say, 'Listen, Officer, this is no time to explain, but do you know that top-secret place in the middle of Hyde Park? Well, he's spying on it! He's a spy!" By now, the guy is fifty yards up Kensington Palace Gardens, looking back anxiously, and he runs off at a fast pace. And I say to the cop, 'Look, he's running off, he's guilty!' And the cop says, 'Now, be off with you, son, be off.' And it was such a deflation that I let go. Then on Monday morning, I came into the Stones office, and Shirley, the secretary there, very Cockney, very down-to-earth, is there, and I say to her, 'Shirley, you'll never guess what happened. There was a spy in the park,' and I tell her the story. And she starts to break up. She laughs and laughs, and I say, 'Shirley, I'm not kidding, I'm serious.' And then she shows me a map of London, and guess what this top-secret copse is! It's a bird sanctuary."

Swales told this story on himself with amusement. But of another incident from his recent past he spoke with a certain shame. "I did something to Anna Freud that I'm not proud of," he said. "I may have gone a bit far." On October 11, 1981, he wrote to Anna Freud to complain that Masson had been "slandering" him in both Europe and America, and, specifically, had been trying to prevent the BBC from hiring him as a consultant on a projected TV series about Freud. Swales asked Anna Freud if she had "authorized Masson to act against me in the systematic manner described," and ended his letter with a request for copies of some letters of Charcot to Freud, of whose existence in Anna Freud's house he had learned from Masson's New Haven lecture. (Swales had several dozen Xerox copies made of the lecture and distributed them in the men's room of the Waldorf-Astoria, where the American Psychoanalytic Association was holding its annual winter meeting. "It was such a bad and stupid paper," he said to me later, "and I wanted people to see what a fool Masson was, and to ask themselves what Anna Freud and Eissler had been up to all those years.") Unknown to Swales, Anna Freud wrote frantically to Eissler on October 19:

I urgently need your help and advice on how I can dissociate myself from this whole Masson-Swales matter. I just got a letter from Peter Swales, a copy of which I am sending you. How can I know what is true and what is fiction, or who is the guilty one or who is innocent? I only know this: I never "commissioned" Masson to proceed against Swales. The main thing is: I wish to have nothing to do with it, neither now nor later. I authorize nothing nor give out copies of letters.

Could it be that Masson made promises in the name of the Archives and allowed access to material that is blocked? I cannot believe that.

To Swales, Anna Freud wrote one of her cool, laconic letters:

Thank you for your letter of October 11th. Please excuse the delay in my answer, which is due to a very busy time here.

You are quite right in assuming that I want to keep out of the dispute between you and Mr. Masson. I think at my age it is too late for disputes.

As regards your wish to have access to certain letters, I am sorry to say that this is not possible at the moment. I have decided that for a time no further such access will be given to anybody, since the consequences are not always what I would wish them to be.

When Swales received this letter, he called a friend of his, Claudia Berman, and asked her if she would send Anna Freud a letter that he would dictate over the telephone. The letter, which Berman duly sent, requested of Anna Freud copies of two letters of Freud to his fiancée about Breuer, which Berman said she needed for research she was doing on Breuer's famous patient Anna O. (Bertha Pappenheim). Anna Freud fell into the trap and promptly sent Berman one of the letters. (The other she withheld as "purely personal.") Then Swales did the thing he is not proud of: he wrote to Anna Freud and gloatingly revealed that Claudia Berman had been a decoy, saying, "It was I who encouraged her to write you. As a matter of fact, I am even responsible for the text of her letter, having drafted it for her over the phone." Eissler knew of the incident—Swales could not resist sending him a copy of his letter to Anna Freud—and brought it up in one of our evening conversations. "That was a terrible thing to do to the poor old lady," he said. "To use a decoy—all right. I have done it myself in my time. But to rub her nose in it—to show her up like that! It was very mean of Swales to do that."

After the Minna Bernays lecture, Swales began to make public further areas of his Freud universe. He gave a lecture at the New School on May 20, 1982, entitled "Freud, Minna Bernays, and the Imitation of Christ," and he privately published a series of papers on such subjects as the influence of cocaine on Freud's concept of the libido, the influence that Johann Weier's 1563 book about witches had on Freud's repudiation of the seduction theory, and Freud's plot to murder Fliess.* He publishes privately by eccentric choice rather

---

* In the murder-plot paper, as in the Minna Bernays lecture, Swales connects a passage in *The Psychopathology of Everyday Life* to a scandalous story told about Freud. It is known (from the testimony of both men) that during their last meeting, in August 1900, in Achensee, in the Tyrol, Freud and Fliess did not get along. They had a peculiar argument about which one of them had first articulated the concept of universal bi-

than out of necessity; several psychoanalytic journals have opened their pages to him, but he prefers to do things his own way. To one of these papers, called "Freud, Martha Bernays, and the Language of Flowers," published in January 1983, Swales appended a postscript that is a kind of credo:

> I am acutely aware when preparing my works that some of them tend to read like *folies à trois* involving Freud, Swales, and the reader. But I console myself with the reflection that the subject of my investigations was an exceedingly bizarre, complex, and devious individual —indeed a man of such masterful artifice that probably to most mortals he will forever remain inscrutable, but

---

sexuality—it was Fliess, as Freud "remembered" a week later—and a more fundamental disagreement about the incompatibility of Fliess's theory of periodicity with psychoanalytic theory. In a book Fliess published in 1906, *In Eigener Sache,* he accused Freud of complicity in the plagiarism of his bisexuality theory by a young Viennese philosopher named Otto Weininger, and recalled the meeting at Achensee, writing that "On that occasion, Freud showed a violence toward me which was at first unintelligible to me. . . . I thought I detected a personal animosity against me on Freud's part which sprang from envy." Swales writes that "privately, to some of his family and to at least one friend, Fliess confided a much more provocative and sinister version of that meeting. . . . According to Fliess, it was Freud's intention to lure him into a lonely mountainous region, then to push him over a precipice or into water below. Fliess claimed he escaped because he had cause to suspect Freud's intention—he was a man of very small stature and he could not swim." Swales adds, "This story, as told, was recovered by my wife and me when interviewing a son of Fliess's close, lifelong friend, Georg Heinitz, in Berlin, and it was confirmed both in essence by Fliess's daughter and in detail, altogether independently, by a niece of Fliess—a daughter of Dr. Oscar Rie, one of Freud's close friends—in an interview with Dr. Frank Hartman." The passage in *Psychopathology* which Swales cites does seem to be about Freud and Fliess in Achensee, and it does have to do with unconscious hostility—but it scarcely corroborates Fliess's fantastical allegation.

especially to those whose conception of psychology, if not general sensibility, has been cast in the reflected image of Freud's theories and who are therefore, of necessity, as it were, prevented from ever seeing through the man.

Needless to say, there is *no way* by which the Freud who emerges in the foregoing pages and in certain other of my works is to be reconciled with, or incorporated into, the standard, received view of the man as "chaste and puritanical," as a scientist of "stern morality" and "flawless integrity.". . . But I am quite content for posterity to judge whose version of the man is the more authentic—whose is the more profound and essential in its fidelity.

In the meantime, I shall continue to expand and to develop the gnostic version of Freud as found in these pages. And if there are readers who, recognizing in this version the *true* Freud, are thankful for it, then I urge them please to give me their moral support.*

The asterisk led to this footnote: ". . . also a little material support. Please wrap $10 (or £5 or 20 DM or 50 FF) in a piece of opaque paper, put the paper in an envelope, and mail it to me at the above address. That way I can continue with publications like this whilst retaining my intellectual and moral independence."

Although Swales leads a bohemian life and is regularly short of cash—"I am the punk historian of psychoanalysis," he once said—he is not entirely without ties to the regular world. After giving the first Minna Bernays lecture, he walked around town and left copies of the lecture at the offices of three well-known New York literary agents. One of them, Georges Borchardt, actually read the lecture, called

Swales the next day to say he would like to take him on, and presently negotiated a contract for the Fliess biography with Random House, for which Swales received a ten-thousand-dollar advance. Borchardt says that in all the thirty years of his agency he has never taken anyone else off the street, as he took Swales.

"There are forty or fifty analysts to whom I send my papers, but I don't write for analysts," Swales told me. "I'm not really interested in what they think. My interests are epistemological. I believe that the Freud and Minna Bernays affair is central to an understanding of Freud's self-analysis, that it's of primary importance in comprehending Freud's intellectual development. That's all I want to say. It's not as if I'm concerned per se with whether Freud had an affair with his silly sister-in-law or not. I built my Freud universe years ago. Today, I plug up a hole or sandpaper it here and there, polish it up. But I did all the work by about 1977. My Freud universe has fermented and brewed, and when I've published everything, 'my Freud'—if I may speak like that —will make more sense to people, will be more internally consistent than the standard Freud. What I'm doing, in a sense, is declaring war on a whole profession—that of psychoanalysis. It can be reduced, in a sense, to my standing up there and saying, 'You don't know what you're talking about. You don't know who this man was. You call yourselves psychologists? You haven't the faintest idea who this man was.' The analysts are utterly ignorant about Freud. They don't know the material, they don't know how the data interlock. Eissler is the one exception. I wish he didn't write in the idiom of psychoanalysis. I wish he wrote just as a psychologist.

"I had a terrible thought about Eissler the other day.

I'll make this awful confession to you, probably at my own expense: If Eissler were to drop dead tomorrow, I'd be a broken man. I'd feel I had nobody left to write for. It's weird. I'd feel cheated if he were to die. I'd think, Oh, God, what's the point of going on?"

PART III

I

He took pleasure in his own speech, in his own thoughts, yes, even in insignificant indifferent actions of everyday life, and was convinced that no one could perform them as well as he. Everything he said and thought possessed a plasticity, a warmth, a quality of importance, which was meant to conceal the lack of deeper substance. For his gifts were not remarkable, he knew little, never delved very deep, and he lacked completely the basic conditions for scientific work: criticism and thoroughness. As a result, his achievements are of moderate value and lack any original content. It was his temperament, his personality, the liveliness and clarity of his presentation which brought about his success. . . . When Weiss talked of a well-known phenomenon, he gave the impression of a great discovery freshly made by him; one could as little help believing in his assertions as one can help laughing when someone else laughs, or yawning when someone else yawns. Much of the high opinion in which people held his ability was inspired by himself, for he was always in the right place, buttonholed everyone, talked only about himself and of himself as the most able expert on the subject with which he just happened to be occupied. Another positive element in his talent was the

quickness with which he thought and his brilliance at
putting two and two together. One could almost say that
his self-confidence was the direct physiological result of
the vivacity, quickness, and clarity of his thought pro-
cesses. He behaved invariably as we would after a lot of
champagne: light, capable, and happy, and with his
incessant restlessness he gave the impression of a raving
maniac. —Freud to Martha Bernays on September 16,
1883, writing about Nathan Weiss, a colleague who had
just hanged himself.

On April 15, 1982, Jeffrey Masson filed a thirteen-
million-dollar lawsuit in the Superior Court of California,
naming Eissler, the Archives, the New-Land Foundation,
and Muriel Gardiner and her grandson Hal Harvey, the
director of the Foundation, as defendants. Masson's lawyer
was James J. Brosnahan, of the large, solid San Francisco
law firm of Morrison & Foerster, whom Masson had approached in November 1981, and who took the case on a
contingency basis, because it interested him. In a twenty-
seven-page complaint, which sometimes reads like *J'Ac-
cuse,* Brosnahan charged Eissler and company with wrongful discharge, breach of implied covenant, breach of duty,
negligent misrepresentation, interference with contractual
relations, conspiracy, intentional infliction of emotional dis-
tress, and libel. "Plaintiff's termination by Defendants was
wrongful and against public policy because it contravened
fundamental policies supporting both freedom of speech, as
guaranteed in the California and federal constitutions, and
the pursuit of historical research and inquiry, which is one
of the enumerated purposes as set forth in the by-laws of the
Archives," Brosnahan wrote, and added, "Rather than pro-

mote historical research, writing, and publication on Freud
and his work, the Defendants have acted, from personal and
private motives, to inhibit, silence, and suppress such scholarship. Among those motives was to conceal from the public
the facts that Freud himself may have recognized that he had
been wrong to abandon completely the 'seduction theory'
and that Defendants' own psychoanalytic views, and hence
their treatment of their patients, needed re-evaluation and
re-examination." (Paradoxically, nowhere does Masson's thesis seem more untenable than in his lawyer's precise and
lucid expression of it. Freud lived to the age of eighty-three.
If he had "recognized that he had been wrong to abandon
completely the seduction theory," why had he given no inti-
mation of this change of mind during the forty-odd years that
followed his repudiation of it?) The lawsuit's charge of libel
referred to Eissler's *cri de coeur* to the *Times*: "Would you
make Director of the Archives someone who writes plain
nonsense?" This, Brosnahan wrote, "was intended by De-
fendant Eissler to expose Plaintiff, and did in fact expose
Plaintiff, to contempt, ridicule, and obloquy," for which he
asked six million dollars in damages.

The suit never came to trial. Masson's prospects hinged
on a ruling as to whether the case should be tried in New
York or in California. In New York, he felt, he stood no
chance whatever, because of New York law on unwritten
contracts; in California, he stood a chance. But since the
ruling would have more probably been for New York—*it*
hinged on whether the headquarters of the Freud Archives
were in Manhattan or in Berkeley—Masson decided to accept
a settlement financed by Muriel Gardiner, who, at the age of
eighty, had felt disinclined to enter into a court battle. He
would receive a hundred and fifty thousand dollars, half to

be paid at the time of the settlement, in August, and half nine months later, in May; for his part, he would return the tapes and documents that Eissler and Anna Freud had given him, and promise not to use in his writings any of the Archives material to which he had had privileged access. Gardiner, who recently wrote a movingly artless and deadpan memoir of her hair-raising activities in the Austrian underground before the outbreak of the Second World War, and who has been the center of a curious and somewhat pointless controversy over whether she was or wasn't the real-life source for Lillian Hellman's *Julia* (Lillian Hellman says she wasn't), has maintained a remarkably evenhanded and forbearing attitude toward Masson. "I liked Masson," she told me in her modest pied-à-terre in a new apartment building on the West Side. Muriel Gardiner grew up in Chicago, the granddaughter of Nelson Morris, who founded one of the giant meat-packing companies, and has been very rich all her life. In her memoir, she writes of a streak of asceticism and a yearning to be socially useful which developed in her character early on and which have marked her life as a psychiatrist, psychoanalyst, political activist, and benefactor. (Among the many objects of her largesse was Freud's famous patient Sergius Pankejeff—better known as the Wolf Man—whom she helped support in Vienna during the last several years of his life, and whose memoirs she translated and edited in 1971.) She is a tall, robust, vigorous woman with white hair who dresses in pants suits and speaks, slowly and deliberately, in well-formed sentences uttered with an old-fashioned upper-class intonation. "Masson and I worked very well together," she went on. "He was energetic. I think he had some right on his side, though he got a little more than he deserved. It was a very emotional business. Kurt Eissler is wonderful, but he doesn't know anything about people. He did so many ill-advised things. He sort of fell in love with this image of the outgoing and unrestrained young man he always wanted to be."

Gardiner went on to tell me of her first meeting with Masson, in 1978 in England, at what Masson has called "a swishy little gathering of the top analysts in the world," which Anna Freud had organized at Hampstead. Masson was there under the wing of Eissler, and Gardiner met him one evening in the bar of the hotel where the world's top analysts were staying. "There were comfortable little tables and comfortable chairs," Gardiner recalled, "and I sat down at a table with two analysts I knew and a young man whom I'd never met before, who turned out to be Jeff. My first impression of him was that he was slick. 'Slick' may be too strong—'facile' may be the right word. He made everything too easy. After a while, the two analysts I knew left for dinner, and Jeff and I stayed and talked for about two hours, and I liked him better. He seemed more serious; he didn't have this too easygoing manner. I soon got the impression, though, that he didn't have the right personality to be an analyst. Analysis was too passive even for me, and Jeff is a much more active and energetic person than I am. I thought, He'd never be satisfied with it and never be good at it. But I didn't tell him this. Several people talked to me afterward about him, and one analyst said, 'I think he's a manipulator.' And I said, 'If he's a manipulator in good causes, then perhaps it doesn't matter.' Another analyst said, 'Oh, he's an opportunist.' I thought, It's interesting that two analysts who are so different from each other—who, in fact, dislike each other—should have the same feeling about him. I always got on well with Jeff alone. His memory was very good. He may not be

the most brilliant scholar in the world, but he's a hard worker
and he's reliable—I mean about appointments and things like
that. But after he dragged me and my grandson into the
suit, I don't think I could be civil to him. A decent person
who considers himself your friend doesn't turn around and
sue you."

2

WHEN I arrived in Berkeley, three months after the
settlement was signed, Masson was in the process of
moving from a house high in the Berkeley hills, where he
had lived with Terri, to new living quarters in the flats below.
The new place was a considerable comedown in every sense
from the old one, which had been a spectacular modern house
with a tree-filled atrium, a swimming pool, a garden, and the
obligatory breathtaking view of the Bay. An Italian journalist
who had interviewed him there had written in *La Repubblica,*
"The forty-year-old Masson reflects in his world—a splendid
house, a Porsche in the driveway—the limpid rationality of
young and modern America, which contrasts with the sombre
Middle European atmosphere in which Freud formulated
his theories." The Porsche had long ago been reclaimed by
the company, and the new place was a small apartment in a
shabby Victorian house—the sort of nondescript, almost-not-
seedy digs typically inhabited by young academics who have
not yet risen very far. When I arrived there, around lunch-
time on a Saturday, Masson's girlfriend, Denise Cammell—
a thin, very pretty woman in her early thirties with a large
amount of fashionably frizzy reddish hair, wearing bluejeans

and an unironed shirt—was in front of the house sweeping, while her daughter, Karima, a sturdy and cheerful eight-year-old, hovered nearby. In the house, there were unpacked cartons everywhere, and an atmosphere of forlornness and homelessness. Masson was in the kitchen heating up, with a nonplussed air, a Stouffer's frozen meal while Simone, a thin, dark, discontented eight-year-old with an interesting face, tried to attract his attention. "Yes, lovey, in a minute," Masson said, scrutinizing the directions on the box. A small, nervous Abyssinian cat named Rama wandered about the apartment with the air of a mental patient. Denise came into the kitchen, sized up the situation (Masson had invited me for lunch), and ran out to the store to buy things for sandwiches. She returned almost instantly, and had lunch on the table almost instantly. Everything Denise did was quick, effective, and pleasant, and she had a warm, easy way with both the girls. She was the owner of two boutiques in Berkeley and of an exercise studio that followed the principles of Jane Fonda. Her father had just lost "all his banks," she said, with a nice mixture of filial rue and self-mockery.

"Denise is *echt* California," Masson said fondly. "When I first met her, you couldn't get more than six words out of her, and they were generally 'like,' 'you know,' 'I mean, like.' She spoke in half sentences. There's something so *echt* California about that."

"It has nothing to do with California," Denise said.

"But you have a basic mistrust of speech, right?"

"It's just not fast enough," Denise said. "It doesn't say what I mean."

During lunch, Denise suddenly turned to Masson and said emotionally. "Those old people—Eissler and Muriel Gardiner—I worry about them. I feel their pain. Eissler knew he was playing with fire when he messed with you, but he couldn't help himself. You're charming—you affect people. You touched Eissler, and you hurt him. I see him bearing the pain. *But you don't feel it, Jeff.* You just don't feel it. I worry about that."

"Denise worries too much," Masson said imperturbably.

"What you did to them, is that—is that *betrayal*?" Denise asked.

"Of course not," Masson said. "What did I do? I gave an interview to the *Times*. Is that reason to destroy a man's career?"

Denise started to say something, and then thought better of it.

"I miss Hanumān," Simone said.

"Yes, lovey," Masson said. "You'll see Hanumān tomorrow, when you spend the night with Mommy." Hanumān was one of the three family dogs, now in Terri's keeping.

After lunch, when Denise had gone back to sweeping the yard, and Simone and Karima had gone off to play in Simone's room, Masson talked about Terri. "She is undoubtedly the most interesting human being I have ever met," he said. "I still love her. I don't think we'll ever come back together. I find her impossible to live with. But she'll always be someone I look up to and respect. She has a fabulous intellect, which she will under no circumstances use anymore. She's Polish. She was in the Warsaw ghetto as a child. When we met, in Toronto, she was a very successful film producer for Canadian television. I persuaded her to quit her job and study philosophy at the university. I got her interested in psychoanalysis, and for many years we worked together, read the analytic literature together, endlessly discussed analytic theory, collaborated on papers. She has a brilliant mind. She really knows how to think. I am not a thinker. I am a fantastic researcher. I love to go to libraries and archives and dig up weird things, but that's all. Terri's mind is like a beautiful machine—to watch it at work is an awesome experience. But she refuses to use it anymore. She is completely disillusioned with psychoanalysis—her analysis was even more disastrous than mine, if that's possible—and with everything else. She rides horseback and studies ballet and absolutely refuses to read a book or talk about anything serious. It's very disturbing to me. She leads a totally disordered life. This is why Simone is with me for the time being. Someone has to get her to school in the morning, and Terri doesn't get up until noon. Someone has to make her meals —Terri says, 'Get her a hot dog.' For the first three years of Simone's life, Terri was an unbelievably perfectionist mother. She was obsessed with taking care of Simone. She would make special food for Simone, she would never let anyone else take care of her. If Simone had a cold, Terri would nurse her as if it was a fatal disease. Then, when Simone was three, it suddenly stopped; it just didn't interest her anymore. When we came to Berkeley, Terri decided she wanted to make money, so she took a job as a headhunter— she found executives for big corporations. She did it so brilliantly that within a few months she was making fifteen thousand dollars a month. We lived very well then. We moved into that big, beautiful house, we bought the Porsche, we had a maid. But then she quit the headhunting business —just like that—and we went from living on fifteen thousand a month to zero, with bills coming in."

Masson's present problem was how to get through the

next six months—after which he would receive the second installment of his settlement. The first half had gone mostly to his lawyer and to taxes. He had not accepted the thirty thousand dollars in severance pay the Archives had offered him. ("I thought it was hush money," he said.) A small advance he had received from the German publishing house Suhrkamp for *The Assault on Truth* was almost gone. He had sent a prospectus of the book to Farrar, Straus & Giroux, where Alice Miller purportedly had influence, but he wasn't very hopeful that a trade publisher would take a book with so many footnotes.

"Never in my life have I had to worry about money the way I am worrying about it now," he said. "They want a thousand dollars at Simone's school, and I don't have a thousand dollars. Until now, there was always a salary coming in. I have been in the university since the age of seventeen, and since the age of twenty-nine I've had a university position. I never had to worry. I now realize how comfortable it all was. The job with the Archives was ideal. I didn't have to teach, I didn't have to see patients, I could travel all over the world, I had lots of prestige, I had money—it was great. Nobody gives up that kind of thing easily."

"But why did you sue Eissler?" I asked. "There are people who are fired from jobs who don't sue."

"What should I have done? Been thankful that he fired me?" Masson said. Then he admitted frankly, "I suppose I did it out of revenge. Eissler had no *business* firing me. You don't *do* that to someone you've been close to. Eissler did to me what Freud did to Ferenczi. This was one of the things I found in Anna Freud's house that appalled me so much. I found evidence of how Freud dumped Ferenczi. I found a packet of letters in Freud's desk between Freud and Jones and Eitingon showing how they had ganged up on Ferenczi and tried to prevent him from reading his last paper at the Wiesbaden conference of 1932. In this paper, called 'Confusion of Tongues Between Adults and the Child,' Ferenczi writes about all the seductions that took place among his patients when they were children. It is a beautiful paper; I think it's my favorite paper in the whole of analytic literature. But Freud couldn't bear to be reminded of seduction. It was like a guilty secret. It reminded him that there was something rotten at the core of psychoanalysis—namely, his abandonment of the seduction theory—and he didn't want to know about it. And Anna Freud and Eissler didn't want to know about it, and they didn't want anyone else to know about it. It was the same thing with my discovery about the Schreber case. That was even more appalling. I found an 1884 article in Freud's library written by Paul Flechsig, Schreber's psychiatrist, which he had personally sent to Freud, reporting that he performed castration experiments on hysterical and obsessional patients in his asylum. This means that when Freud wrote his essay on Schreber he knew that castrations had taken place in the asylum where Schreber was held, but he still could write that Schreber suffered from the *delusion* that the great Paul Flechsig wanted to castrate him. I think Freud was a great and remarkable thinker, but *he wasn't honest*. He was a man who just lost his courage. His entire theory after he abandoned seduction was the product of moral cowardice, because Freud knew that Schreber was in an asylum where they were trying to castrate him, and he never mentions it. Now, what would you say about somebody like that? No matter how brilliant he is, how good a thinker he is, he is not being honest if he omits that fact from his essay."

"That's a very serious charge against Freud," I said. (Later, it occurred to me to wonder if Flechsig had not sent Freud the article *after* Freud had published his essay on Schreber; when Flechsig's article first appeared, Freud was an obscure young neurologist, to whom an eminent psychiatrist was not apt to send complimentary reprints.)

"There aren't too many interpretations possible of my discovery," Masson said grimly. "I think Eissler would have admitted that I was right. I think if I had said to him, 'Look, I'm never going to make this public—this is just between you and me—but just take a look at this,' he would have said, 'Yes, you're right. But never, never tell the goyim.' I swear that's what he would have said. 'Never let it out; it's just between the two of us. We can know this. We're strong enough to digest it. But for anybody else it would be the beginning of the end of psychoanalysis.' It would have been like Dostoyevski's Grand Inquisitor."

"Did Eissler ever tell you that there were certain things that had to be kept from the goyim?" I asked.

"No," Masson said, and abruptly changed his tack. "If Eissler had ever told me that I must keep quiet about certain things, I never would have accepted the job with the Archives. I figured that Eissler was like me—that he didn't care, that he wanted the truth to come out, however damaging to the profession it might be."

"But didn't you suspect, knowing how Eissler reveres Freud, that he couldn't tolerate hearing anything said against him?"

"No, I didn't think that. I thought he *could* tolerate it.

I thought he was like me. What difference does it make to him or to me what Freud did or didn't do? He's not our father. With Anna Freud, I could understand it. But for Eissler to feel that way—I thought he was too intelligent for that."

"You should have read him more carefully."

"Yes, perhaps. But he chose me for the job. If he had wanted a hagiographer of Freud, there were thousands of people he could have chosen. But he chose me. He knew I was not like those other people. He was warned about me by just about everyone who had ever met me. And still he chose me."

"So maybe the question isn't why he fired you but why he hired you."

"That's right. When I was in France last month, somebody said to me, '*M. Masson, si l'on est un lapin, on n'invite pas un renard à dîner*'—if you are a rabbit, you don't invite a fox to dinner. 'Now, you are a fox,' this man said, 'and the analysts are rabbits. Why did they invite you into their warren?' And it's a good question. What *was* Eissler's idea in making me his successor? It puzzles me even now."

The telephone rang, and Masson answered it in the next room. When he returned, he sighed, and said, "Alice Miller —she's just like my mother, I swear. I feel guilty about her. She's here in Berkeley, she has nothing to do, and I feel I ought to do more for her. I like her," he added defensively.

"Eissler and I had a wonderful time together," he went on, "and I still love him—I really do. After the Board voted not to renew my contract, he wrote me a long letter. It's an incredible letter, a kind of love letter. I got it out of my files to show you, but now I'm not sure I ought to show it to you." Masson deliberated, and then went and got the letter. "You might as well see it," he said, and he handed me the letter, which read, in part:

Dear Professor Masson,

I guess the moment draws nearer when your official connection with the Sigmund Freud Archives will be terminated, and I guess that our friendship will go down the drain at the same time. Both started full of promise and with an outlook of constructive coöperation, and both seem to end in disaster.

My friend and teacher August Aichhorn always said that when two people part they should part in such a way that they can greet each other when they meet later. I do not know for certain: shall we greet each other when we meet again, or shall we look aside, in different directions? ...

I am sure I mentioned in conversation with you that from my 30th year of life I never did anything for another person with a view to receiving later acknowledgment or gratitude. In this case, I beg to be permitted an exception. Have you ever had another friend who was not only ready to give but also actually gave you, at the mere mention of a desired favor or a request, as much as I did, with pleasure and without asking for any reciprocity? If you have had one, give me his name, I should like to meet him.

Now everything I got for you has turned into shambles, and I know I shall never be able to convince you that you have destroyed it unnecessarily and wantonly. I shall not repeat my arguments because they fall on deaf ears anyway.

You will recall that I informed you loyally and faithfully whenever I was told that you were indiscreet, dishonest, an inefficient historian, gossipy, bragging, etc. All these accusations and suspicions were rejected by me, because I loved you and believed in you.

When the two unfortunate interviews were published in the New York *Times,* I tried to deny that you had committed a terrible gaffe. Only after hearing from one Board member after another that they had been shocked by the interviews, and after repeatedly rereading the second one, I had no argument left in your defense. I was forced to drop the praise with which I had introduced you to the Board in 1980, and had to admit that I had been mistaken. . . .

However, I do not want to reproach you, although I think with bitterness about what is going on. I carry the full responsiblity. I am the older and the more experienced one of us two, and I should have recognized that you were not the proper person for the functions in which I desired so much to see you active. I reproach myself that I permitted myself to believe in you, although I was warned by many people—frankly, by almost everyone who knows you. But all of us are stubborn at times, and I steadfastly declared that what people said about you could not possibly be true. I still think they may be wrong, although I have had such a high price to pay for having trusted you and your abilities, your charm, your wit, your affection. *Tant pis.* . . .

Do you remember our first meeting? Already at that time you broached the question of a complete edition of the Fliess letters. Do you remember that I told you I feared that Anna Freud would not agree to it, because her father's letters have been regularly used to diminish his character, or for like purposes? Do you recall what a certain Professor Masson answered?

Do you recall that Anna Freud after a conversation

with you repeated the same premonition? Did you not reassure me that this could never happen, so far as you were concerned, because you admired Freud like no one else, and the complete edition would only show him in his full glory, etc.

Well, of course, after studying the letters you may have changed your mind regarding Freud's character. You were in no position to foresee your later opinion when you started your work. But you must admit you broke the promise you had given and did exactly what Anna Freud feared might happen again. . . .

My original draft of this letter ended with the statement that the fiery sign of *"Mene mene tekel upharsin"* should appear on the wall of your study, because you broke your solemn promise and caused Anna Freud heartache and disappointment, but I was told that you would probably not have enough sense of humor to tolerate such an ending and might feel provoked by it.

I do not know how to end. Should I write "with best wishes"? "Sincerely"? "Truly yours"? "Let bygones be bygones"? I do not know.

K. R. Eissler, M.D.

3

THE day before I was to return to New York, I paid a call on Victor Calef in his San Francisco office. Calef, a squat, dark-complexioned older analyst, with bluntly etched features and a tough, no-nonsense manner, told me bitterly, "Jeff rejected me. I don't need that." He had little to say about Masson's position on the seduction theory; in fact, he seemed rather foggy about exactly what that position was. The same could be said of all the other analysts I spoke to who had been friendly with Masson and were no longer on speaking terms with him. In every case, it was a personal issue—not ideology—that had caused the breach. Calef had felt wounded and slighted when Masson backed out of a Festschrift that Calef had organized for his former teacher and idol, the Freud scholar Siegfried Bernfeld, and had planned to have printed in a small professional journal. A large art photograph of Bernfeld in profile hung on a wall of Calef's office, and whenever Calef mentioned his name he would glance over at the photograph, as if Bernfeld himself were in the room. Calef told me that Masson had worked with him in the early stages of the Festschrift project but had then withdrawn, saying that he had bigger fish to fry than to write for a little local journal. "It was a rejection of me," Calef said. "I was hurt. I felt like a fool." He added, "It was a great loss for me. I was very taken with him. At my age, to lose any friend is difficult." Another San Francisco analyst, Edward Weinshel, with whom Masson had been on equally friendly terms, said that his relationship with Masson had effectively ended when Masson failed to write or call after Weinshel's wife died. Masson himself told me of the trouble he had got into with a Berkeley analyst— a distinguished older European woman named Anna Maenchen—when he complained to a young woman he had met at a party about having to "drag this old bat Anna Maenchen with me on the plane to Europe." Unfortunately, the young woman turned out to be a patient of Anna Maenchen's; during a session, she quoted Masson's words, and Anna Maenchen never forgave him.

After seeing Calef, I dropped in at the house of Robert

Goldman, the chairman of the Department of South and Southeast Asian Studies at Berkeley and Masson's best friend. Goldman, an attractive, bearded, fast-talking, very smart and funny man, who went to Erasmus Hall High School, in Brooklyn, had met Masson in India fifteen years ago, when both were Ph.D. candidates. He and his wife, Laurie, an artist, also originally from New York, served me coffee and cake in their living room and talked about Masson with the sort of affectionate derision with which one will speak of a lovable but endlessly troublesome pet. Laurie Goldman said that it was impossible to have Masson over for dinner with other people, because of the way he monopolized the conversation. "He has to be the center of attention at all times," she said, "or he goes to sleep." The Goldman household (there were two small boys, Seth and Jesse) reminded me of the pleasant, orderly, art- and book-filled households of youngish academics and professionals on the upper West Side of New York. "Jeff is a connoisseur of rejection," Goldman said. "He has few friends. He falls out with everyone eventually. He goes through people. If he had wanted, he could be in Anna Freud's house now. He gets depressed and bored when things are going smoothly. He needs chaos and trouble and excitement." Of Masson's work in Sanskrit, Goldman said, "He's an outstanding Sanskrit scholar—one of the finest of his generation. He cuts through mounds of traditional *dreck* to find something fresh and alive. But he's careless. He makes small, foolish errors that leave him open to attack, and that people who don't like his ideas pounce on. That devastating review by Richard Gombrich is a case in point."

Wendy O'Flaherty, Masson's old enemy at Harvard, who is now a professor in the University of Chicago's Divinity School and a widely published and highly regarded Sanskritist, agreed with Goldman's assessment of Masson's scholarship when I talked with her on the telephone. "I think Jeff is a good Sanskritist," she said. "It's not impossible to be a good Sanskritist, and it doesn't necessarily take brilliance to be a good Sanskritist. It takes a kind of knack for the language, and it also takes a lot of hard work. Jeff had both of those capacities, and some of the work he has done is very good work, like his book on Abhinavagupta's aesthetics. But he is so mean, and I think the meanness spoils the work. I have trouble dealing with his hatred of everything, and with his anger. He's full of self-hate of a very complicated kind. I don't know anyone whom Jeff loves. I don't even know anyone Jeff likes. I can't imagine being friends with Jeff. I can't imagine anyone being friends with Jeff. I touch certain nerves in him that may make him even meaner to me than he is to everybody else. I gather from other people that he's not nice to anybody, but he certainly has always been beastly to me. I wouldn't sleep with Jeff, and he might have regarded that as a kind of gauntlet."

4

I WAS leaving San Francisco for New York on an evening plane, and that afternoon Masson and I had a final meeting, in my hotel room. Earlier, I had spotted him and Alice Miller in the hotel dining room and had joined them for a few minutes. Alice Miller spoke dourly of her conviction that ninety percent of all women who come into psychotherapy were sexually abused as children. "Isn't that figure very high?" I asked. "It is a modest estimate," she said darkly. Later, in my room, Masson went on with the subject. "There you have the kernel of disagreement between me and every orthodox analyst. Orthodox analysts say, 'We can't do anything about the past, we can't help the fact that your father raped you when you were five.' That sounds reasonable enough, but it's so easy to slide from this position into saying, 'It doesn't matter whether he did or not; the important thing is your feelings about it.' Which is not reasonable. There's an enormous difference between whether you were beaten within an inch of your life and whether you imagined you were. There's an enormous difference between whether you actually were in Auschwitz and whether you dreamed you were in Auschwitz. And it's not the fantasies that we have to look at first; it's the reality. Freud originally believed that, and he did always have a certain pull in that direction. He was never comfortable with having given up the seduction theory. It bothered him all his life. It was as if he were haunted by a piece of intellectual dishonesty, because with every patient he's ever written about —the Wolf Man, the Rat Man, Dora—he keeps coming back to the question of fantasy versus reality."

I said, "You know, as you've been talking I've had the feeling that you're bored with what you're saying. You're making yourself go through the paces, but none of this interests you very much anymore."

"Right," Masson said. "It doesn't. It's no longer new to me. I've discovered it. I know it. I don't want to spend the rest of my life explaining what I know. I'm finished with psychoanalysis. I want to get on to something new. I'm quick. I understand things quickly, and I get bored easily. When I've understood something, I don't want to have it repeated to me a hundred times. Even the way I drive. I can't bear to drive in Berkeley. The light turns green. The other drivers look at it, they think about it, they say to their companions, 'The light has turned green. That means we can move now. Let us proceed.' In France, the light turns green and fifty cars move. Most people, having discovered one letter of Fliess to Freud, would stay with it for the next twenty years. They wouldn't discover anything new. Just having gone to Anna Freud's house would be sufficient for them. Not for me. Once I was there and found what I wanted, it would have been time to get on to something else, to search for new things. I was always searching for new things. I got bored with Sanskrit. I found what I thought were the most interesting things in Sanskrit—I put them all in my book *The Oceanic Feeling*—and that was it. I thought, If I continue in Sanskrit, I'll always be working over the same material—and I didn't want that. I wanted new territory. I found it with Freud. And now I feel I've come to the end of that, too. I wouldn't feel that way if I were in Anna Freud's house and had everyone's confidence. Then I would be going through the house with a fine-tooth comb, looking for important new material. But since I can't, I feel there is nothing further for me to do in that field. *Assault on Truth* will be my swan song. It doesn't mean that it will be the end of me—only of my interest in psychoanalysis. I'll move on to something totally different."

"What will you do?" I asked.

"I really don't know," Masson said. "I had this idea of doing a book on love, which everyone who knows me tells me is a terrible idea. Bob Goldman, Terri, Denise—they all say it's junk. I guess I don't have that much to say about love. There's another idea I had when Terri and I were still together—that she and I and Simone would go around the world, staying for a couple of months in each country and finding out what's wrong with each culture. I feel I have unique insights into the evils of different societies, and I feel if I had someone like Terri with me I could collect about twenty-five countries and show how if you grow up in this country and that culture your life will be distorted in such-and-such a way. But who is interested in that? It's not a very constructive thing to do."

"But you don't like doing constructive things," I said.

"No, I don't. I don't think there's anything constructive to do. I hate books that say how wonderful something is. I see that for people who are truly smart, like Bob Goldman, there really isn't much they want to do, or can do. The truly smart people seem to do less and less. It's terrible. The dull have taken over. All the books I read today—they're junk. I can't find anything to read in any field. I've stopped reading the analytic journals. There's nothing in them anymore, nothing whatever. In the fifties, there were at least a few things you could read."

"You have, as they say, decathected from analysis," I said. "There isn't anyone in the profession whom you care about anymore. When you were fascinated by analysts, you found the analytic journals interesting enough."

"I was a fool then," Masson said. "I can hardly believe some of the things I did and felt in those days. I remember a dinner party at our house where we had invited a lot of so-called important analysts. I desperately wanted to be recognized as somebody of consequence, and it was my fantasy that the phone would ring and somebody really distinguished would be on the line for me. And, sure enough, in the middle of dinner the phone rang, and the maid—we had a maid then—came in and said, 'There's a Dr. Eissler on the phone.' Everybody exchanged looks, and I was so pleased I could have fainted. I said to the maid, 'Tell him I'm having dinner and will call him later.' I could have clapped my hands in glee. Now, what a totally childish, adolescent reaction that was! Today, I would go ten blocks out of my way to avoid speaking to an analyst. There are no duller people in the world than analysts—except, possibly, Sanskritists."

"You're in a kind of depression," I said.

"But I'm not. When I was at that meeting of the Archives Board, and all those people were there, I listened to them, and I thought, God, they're real bores. I didn't care if anybody agreed or disagreed with me. But I knew those thirteen people were bores. They didn't have anything interesting to say."

"Nothing *is* interesting. We invest certain things with interest."

"*No.* Certain things *are* objectively interesting, and certain things are *not.* I'm always interested when people come up with something I didn't know. Even Alice Miller. In some ways, she's quite an ordinary person, but she does manage to say things that are interesting. Eissler was interesting. He had peculiar ideas about dreams, about all kinds of things. He was not boring, and for a while he was fascinated with what I was discovering, but in the end he turned out to be a company man. I think that the best people in any field eventually become disillusioned and withdraw from the field. I'd like to find some way to avoid that. I don't want to withdraw. I don't want to become cranky and eccentric and paranoid—which I don't consider myself yet—but I can certainly see myself going in that direction. Terri's solution was just to forget everything intellectual and start dancing. She studies ballet. Well, at forty-five she can't become a great ballet dancer. She rides horses. She developed a disdain for the world of ideas, in which there was nobody as good as she was. She's the smartest person I've ever met. She thought better than I did. Anything I said, she'd go a step further. Bob Goldman is a little bit like that, and he's bored with everything, too. Nothing really interests him, either. Not even these historical ideas of mine. He hears them for the first time and says 'Yes, isn't that interesting?,' and that's it. He'll never pursue it. He's a very pessimistic man."

5

A FEW days after my return to New York, Masson, in a state of elation, telephoned me to say that Farrar, Straus & Giroux had taken *The Assault on Truth*. "Wait till it reaches the best-seller list, and watch how the analysts will crawl," he crowed. "They move whichever way the wind blows. They will want me back, they will say that Masson is a great scholar, a major analyst—after Freud, he's the greatest analyst who ever lived. Suddenly they'll be calling, begging, cajoling: 'Please take back what you've said about our profession; our patients are quitting.' They'll try a short smear campaign, then they'll try to buy me, and ultimately they'll have to shut up. Judgment will be passed by history. There is no possible refutation of this book. It's going to cause a revolution in psychoanalysis. Analysis stands or falls with me now."

Over the next months, Masson often called me to keep

me abreast of developments with *The Assault on Truth* and with the complete Freud-Fliess correspondence, which Harvard seemed to be hanging back from publishing. In May 1983, he received the second seventy-five thousand dollars of his settlement with the Archives, and wrote Eissler a long letter of self-justification and recrimination, which Eissler never answered. In June, Harvard accepted the Freud-Fliess letters, paid Masson four thousand dollars, and scheduled publication for the fall of 1984. In September, Masson was expelled from the Canadian Psychoanalytic Society (and thus automatically from the International Psycho-Analytical Association) for non-payment of dues. In October, I spoke to Wendy O'Flaherty again. She asked me what Masson was doing. I told her he had written a book that he expected to be a best-seller.

"That's what he's making money on," O'Flaherty said impatiently. "I mean, what does he care about in life? If he's bored with Sanskrit and with psychoanalysis—both of which I think are infinitely interesting—what has he found to care about in their place?"

I said I didn't think he had found anything, and added, "I wonder if he has ever cared about anything."

O'Flaherty said, "When I was little, I remember how astonished and interested I was in how easy it is to take life —when you're driving a car, all you have to do is move the wheel a few inches to the left and you kill somebody and also die yourself—and how difficult it is to keep alive someone who is sick. Building is interesting, because it's ultimately impossible, I suppose, but killing is boring. It's easy to see through something—to show how stupid it is, or how wrong—but that doesn't take very long, and then you're finished. If you want to show how boring India is, and how stupid it is, and how wrong Freud was, and how stupid analysts are, that doesn't take more than a year or two. I think that's the way it has been with Jeff—not so much not caring about anything but caring only to kill. Killing may be amusing while it lasts, but it never lasts very long, and you are back where you started. Killing doesn't solve the problem of boredom."

In September, I sent Masson a book by Marshall Berman, another schoolmate of his at Harvard—a study of the social origins of modernism, called *All That Is Solid Melts into Air*. A few weeks later, I received this reply:

Many thanks for sending me the book by Marshall. I was, I confess, struck by how much I have changed in views over the years. I cannot read something like this anymore without distaste. I can't bear these "large" comparisons and broad comments. The naming of names is also very tiresome, page after page. In short, I am convinced, yet again, that there is little left to read. But it was nice of you to send it to me, and it gave me yet another opportunity to wonder about old cathexes and transferences.

I have begun working on my next book: "Attitudes Toward Women and Children in Nineteenth-Century European Psychiatry." I drive down to Stanford every Thursday and work in the Lane Medical Library. I have selected 842 volumes of pediatric, gynecological, and psychiatric French and German medical journals, and read them through, cover to cover, from 1880–1900, looking for interesting material. It's working. For example, yesterday I found the ice-penis: a gynecologist invented a special machine (the size and shape of a penis) that sends very cold water into the female vagina. There are pictures of it, and elaborate case histories. But I must confess that when I began looking over the journals, and realized that I was now dealing only with printed sources —that there would be no envelopes tumbling out of the bookshelves filled with old and unknown letters from Freud—I became depressed. Simply nothing can take the place of being the first person to look at a new document and realize its significance. Books are not the same as letters. Not that I am sorry for what I did, only sorry that I never got the opportunity to go through Anna Freud's house really carefully. Even now I like to fantasize about what I would have found. I know that such an opportunity will never come again, and it makes me a little sad.

ABOUT THE AUTHOR

JANET MALCOLM was born in Prague. She was educated at the High School of Music and Art, in New York, and at the University of Michigan. She is on the staff of *The New Yorker* and lives in Manhattan with her husband and daughter. Her previous books are *Diana and Nikon: Essays on the Aesthetics of Photography* and *Psychoanalysis: The Impossible Profession.*